Given in Memory of

Ira Stuart Pflueger

by

Mrs. Henry Dendahl

1976

$5.95

The Naming of Persons

By Paul Tournier

The Adventure of Living
A Doctor's Casebook in the Light of the Bible
Guilt and Grace
The Healing of Persons
Learn to Grow Old
The Meaning of Persons
The Naming of Persons
The Person Reborn
A Place for You
The Whole Person in a Broken World

Paul Tournier

The Naming of Persons

1817

HARPER & ROW, PUBLISHERS

New York, Evanston, San Francisco, London

Translated by Edwin Hudson from the French
Quel nom lui donnerez-vous?
Labor et Fides S.A., Geneva 1974

THE NAMING OF PERSONS is published in England under the title
WHAT'S IN A NAME?.

FIRST U.S. EDITION

ISBN: 0-06-068371-6

LIBRARY OF CONGRESS CATALOG CARD NUMBER: 74-25710

75 76 77 78 79 10 9 8 7 6 5 4 3 2 1

Contents

1 Giving a Name   1

2 The Problem of Possessiveness   31

3 Why This Name?   63

4 The Mother's Voice   91

   Notes   113

I

Giving a Name

I meet an old friend in the street. He says some kind things about my last book, on the problems of retirement and old age. He is a little younger than I am, and he tells me about his own experience. Before we part, he suddenly asks,

'Are you working on another book for us?'

'Yes, I'm just starting on one, actually.'

'Good. What's it on?'

'It's on giving names to children.'

He seems quite surprised. He frowns thoughtfully and gives me a questioning look. I explain: Pastor Alain Perrot suggested the subject to me many years ago. I was one of his parishioners at the time, in Champel. I was surprised myself at first. But I soon realized that what was involved was the person of the child, his individual identity and the respect due to him even before his birth.

The constant theme of my writings has been the human person and its inalienable value: the person of the patient and also that of the doctor; the person of the husband and of the wife; that of the aged, in my last book; and now

3

the person of the child. I think that many of the problems of our time, such as the spiritual loneliness experienced by so many people, or the boredom induced by our technical civilization, denounced by the young, come from the fact that we attach too much importance to things and not enough to persons.

Before I started my book my wife and I invited Pastor Alain Perrot to come and see us, so that we could talk over his idea and get a better understanding of what he had in mind. At the end of our conversation he told us a story that is worth repeating here.

When he was five or six years old he was invited to a children's party. There happened to be another boy there with the same name – Alain. This other Alain was puzzled and even annoyed – he had always thought, up till then, that he was the only Alain in the world. He looked upon his Christian name as his exclusive property. And now here was another boy who had somehow stolen it. He felt as if he had been robbed of his identity.

Later in life when the second Alain was to be married, he asked Pastor Alain Perrot to perform the ceremony. The Pastor then reminded him of their first meeting, which the other had quite forgotten.

I was delighted with this childhood incident, because it aptly illustrates the role of the name in the development of the person. When I say that I am a person I am expressing two things that seem to be contradictory, but in fact are complementary: one is that I am an original human being, not to be confused with any other; a unique being, always himself despite his disconcerting diversity, as

4

Rousseau so aptly says. On the other hand I am stating that I am not an isolated individual, complete in myself, but that I exist only in virtue of my relationship with others, with the world of which I am a part. The word 'person' thus involves two movements, of separation and of union.

What separates and distinguishes me from other people is the fact that I am called by my name; but what unites me with them is the very fact that they call me. The movement of separation is what we understand by the formation of the self. Gradually the child must learn to recognize himself as distinct, first from his mother, then from other people, and finally from the world which he perceives as increasingly large and complex. But the very fact that he is addressed and has to respond constitutes a movement of union.

Professor Richard Siebeck, a doctor from Heidelberg, expressed this perfectly when he said, 'It is the calling that creates the person.' Such was the first human experience described in the Bible: when Adam, seized with remorse and fear, was hiding in the darkest thickets of the garden of Eden, he heard Yahweh's voice calling him by name: 'Adam, Adam, where are you?' (Gen. 3.9).

This passage shows that the unique value and dignity of the human person came from God, from the fact that God speaks to him as to a partner in a dialogue, a being whom he has created in his own image, and whom he calls upon to respond to him, whom he thus makes responsible before him. This is the very basis of the notion of the person, as Dr Aloys von Orelli points out:

'God has not placed man in the world as an anonymous and interchangeable element, but has called him by his name.'[1]

As the prophet Isaiah puts it:

Yahweh called me before I was born,
from my mother's womb he pronounced my name (Isa. 49.1).

God does not call only prophets and believers, but all men. This is expressed again by Isaiah when he attributes to Yahweh these words spoken to Cyrus the barbarian, the enemy of his people:

I have called you by your name,
. . . though you do not know me (Isa. 45.4).

The Bible does not put forward abstract theories about the human person. It is anecdotal, it tells of what has happened to real men in the context of their actual lives. And so it is full of proper names, as you will surely have noticed. There are whole pages of proper names, of genealogies which are carefully printed in every edition, but which we willingly skip in reading. Nevertheless, this abundance of names has a meaning – that the Bible is concrete and personal, that God speaks to each individual personally. Note, too, with what tenderness St Paul, at the conclusion of his letters, after pages of abstruse intellectual teaching, turns to mentioning individuals, calling each by his name.

I like that, because the doctor too works in concrete situations in which he discovers the importance of the person, not as a general proposition, but for each individual in particular. Thus he is made aware day by day of the fundamental need of all men to be recognized as persons, the struggle they must engage in from childhood to old age to get themselves treated as persons rather than things to be possessed, exploited, used, despised, manipulated, bought and sold. It is a fact, for example, that there is less absenteeism among artisans working under their own names than among workers incorporated into an anonymous mass.

The child, then, must from the start become aware of himself as a person. It is through his personal name that he will come to this awareness. Your child will hear his name, the name you chose for him in advance — Francis, perhaps — many thousands of times throughout his life, and he will know that it means him, an individual, responsible for his own feelings and actions.

Obviously he will hear his name spoken in all sorts of ways. Long before he learns to talk and understand grown-up speech he will hear it spoken tenderly, when his mother caresses him and lovingly repeats his name: 'Little Francis, my treasure!' He understands the caress very well, and already the name that is associated with it is stored for ever in the mysterious engrams of his memory. Then his mother will play with him, hiding her face and asking, 'Where has Francis gone to? He's not there!' Then uncovering her face she will exclaim, 'Peekaboo! There's Francis!' And Francis will chuckle with pleasure.

Later, even before he has learnt to say 'I want', he may be saying 'Francis wants'. Do not imagine that he is speaking in the third person as lackeys and kings used to; he is in fact using his name in the first person. In naming himself he is asserting his existence.

But he will also hear his name used interrogatively: 'Francis, do you love your mommy?' Or commandingly: 'Francis, eat your soup!' Or reproachfully: 'Naughty Francis!' And now his name, instead of being accompanied by a caress, is punctuated with a slap.

He will go on hearing his name spoken in every possible tone of voice: 'Francis, you are silly!' 'Well done, Francis, I'm proud of you!' 'Francis, don't touch that!' 'Francis, you are getting on my nerves with your continual questions!' 'Don't cry, Francis!' 'Francis, say thank you.' Obviously I am exaggerating a little, because, thanks to the psychologists, methods of bringing up children have changed to some extent. But he will still hear his name when he returns home after staying out late with his friends, and hears his mother anxiously calling, 'Francis, Francis, where are you?' And he will realize how much he is loved despite the scolding he receives.

Again, it is this same Christian name of his that he will hear uttered softly and passionately, when the time comes for some girl to murmur as she offers him her lips, 'Francis, I do love you!' His name will always be associated with the 'you', the 'Thou' of which Martin Buber wrote,[2] and which he contrasts with the 'It' of the thing; for it is the 'Thou', the 'you', which characterizes the personal relationship.

When I call someone by his Christian name I am expressing the intimacy that exists between us. Above all

I am making him feel that I am addressing his person and not his function or his social personage. I recall an incident that took place a good number of years ago. We had just arrived for a religious conference. Through a mistake in the administrative office, Nelly, my wife, went into the room we had been allotted, only to find it already occupied by one of my friends, the well-known theologian Emile Brunner. She began to apologize, but he cut her short:

'Who are you?'

'I'm Paul Tournier's wife . . .'

'I know,' he said. 'I know you are Paul Tournier's wife. But who are you, yourself? What is your name?'

'Nelly.'

'Good! I'm Emile. We're going to use "tu" to each other, aren't we?'

In introducing herself as my wife, she had been playing the conventional social game. The use of the Christian name marks a change in the relationship, the personalization of the relationship. A wife may sometimes come to ask herself whether she is really accepted as herself in a community, and not just as the wife of her husband.

There are communities all of whose members use 'tu' to each other and call each other by their Christian names, such as Jean Vanier's Arche, and M. Rohrbach's JEAN Association. Some surgeons make a practice of using 'tu' to their patients, perhaps an instinctive acknowledgment that they hold their lives in their hands. My colleague Francesco Racanelli, of Florence, uses 'tu' with everybody, with that Italian spontaneity of his. In

9

the clinic run by my colleague Walther Lechler in Herrenalb, the patients, the doctors and all the staff use Christian names to each other. This obviously demands a very real and profound personal commitment if it is not to turn into another social convention.

Modern English no longer makes the distinction between the familiar 'thou' and the polite 'you', which is still made in other languages, such as French with its 'tu' and 'vous'. Its place is taken by the use of the Christian name, which the Americans in particular are quick to use as soon as any personal relationship is formed. But there again the frequency of the usage tends to attenuate its intimate significance.

The name, then, is of great importance. It is the key to effective relationship between two partners, both for the one who is named and for the other who uses his name in speaking to him. Well before he begins to talk, the child registers names in his memory. He knows quite well who is meant when he hears 'There's Mommy' or 'Here's Daddy'. The first word he says is likely to be 'Mommy'. For him it is not a common noun, but a proper name. Listen to the child who has got lost in a big store. In the office they ask him,

'What is your name?'

'Francis.'

'Francis what?' they ask, wanting to know his surname.

But Francis does not know. So they ask him,

'What's your mommy called?'

And Francis replies, 'She's called Mommy.'

As time goes by the child learns to name persons and things. His discovery of the world goes precisely in step with his learning of names. And this is true of his whole life. Later on he will still be distinguishing between the people whom he really knows, whom he has met and whose names he uses, and those he knows only by sight. When I am introducing people to each other I say their names, and the two people will thereafter be able to say that they 'know each other'. Perhaps at the end of their conversation one of them will say to the other, 'Would you mind telling me your name again? I didn't quite catch it when we were introduced.'

Sometimes the name that has been given may be the thing that turns the conversation on to a more personal level – 'Ah! I once had a teacher of that name. He used to persecute me. I hated school because of him!' And so confidences begin.

Or else, hearing that his new acquaintance is called Ivan, rather than John, Jean or Juan, the other will exclaim, 'But that's a Russian name!' 'Yes, my mother was of Russian origin. I have wonderful memories of her. I was called after her father. My grandfather was a general,' he adds, drawing himself up.

'Why was I given the name Virgil?' writes Gheorghiu.[3] It is because the Romanians are proud of their Latin origin: 'As soon as you enter Romania you hear Roman names – Trajan, Livia, Virgil, Cicero, Lucia, Aurelian, Olive and Horace.'

The child does not only learn names, he invents them himself, lots of them, and so creates his own personal world. He has his own way of naming his mother, his brothers and sisters, his grandparents, and his friends. He gives names to all his possessions, and he possesses everything that he names – his teddy-bear, his doll, his tricycle or a favourite corner to which he loves to go and where he feels really at home.

Like primitive man he thus personifies animals, objects and imaginary powers. For primitive man also, writes Georges Gusdorf,[4] 'the significance of the name . . . is linked with the very essence of the thing . . . To know the name of a thing is to have power over it.' And he quotes the work of Jean Piaget on the child's period of nominal realism: for the child, it is 'a way of appropriating to himself everything that he is capable of naming'. So the child invents words and names in order to enrich his world. He is fond of secret languages and secret names, because his possessions are more personal to himself if the names he gives them are known only to him.

Secret languages! We are touching on the child's great treasure, the land of make-believe, the stories he tells himself, in which he plays a part as he tells them, always adding new episodes. They are real personal possessions, because no one else knows about them. He gives names to all the people who inhabit this make-believe world, and also to the countries and places into which it transports him. These names are very important. They are what give reality to all these imaginary adventures.

The child has difficulty in distinguishing between fiction and reality simply because the people he invents exist for him as names, just as real people do. He even has a more personal communication with them, since it is he who has given them their names, rather than having names imposed from outside by society. I remember getting a letter from a former patient, in which she showed her great confidence in me by telling me about some of her childhood dreams. There were pages and pages of them, with all the names given. And what names! What poetry, what ingenuity, what imagination, what fantasy filled those pages! When one thinks of the difficulties experienced by the manufacturers of perfumes, patent medicines and detergents, in finding attractive names for their products, one cannot but admire the rich creative talent of the child.

To make a character live, you have to give him a name – a common noun is insufficient. It is a point worth underlining. In his book on aggression[5] Konrad Lorenz describes the calls used by certain animals and birds to proclaim sovereignty over their territory. Heinroth, he says, states that the crowing of the cock means to him 'That is a cock!' But he points out that Bäumer, by far the greatest expert on gallinaceous birds, detects a more precise message: 'That is the cock Balthazar!'

The actors in children's make-believe are like that. They are living and personal, because they have proper names. Not just a cock, but the cock Balthazar. None of the names invented by the child for his characters is unimportant. Each is charged with a certain magic power, each evokes a certain association of ideas, which may be extremely ingenious, and each arouses strong emotions.

How prodigious is the imagination of the child, which

can conjure up worlds without number, exciting adventures and faces with striking features. And this flood of names and pictures leads him on to invent games in which to act out his myths, and to give new meanings to the quite ordinary objects he finds about him.

Throughout his life, the positivist culture of school, followed by the daily routine of work, will stifle this overflowing of natural fantasy. At school, if he loses himself in his dream, he is scolded; he is letting his attention wander, and not listening to the teacher, who is talking about things that matter. Later on he will be a good doctor or a good workman only if he thinks about nothing but his work. Being concerned as I am now with old people, I see the result. Those who are dying of boredom, those who do not know what to do with the leisure time that retirement brings, are the ones who have had their creative imagination ground out of them by the mill of school and work. What a contrast with the child who peopled his mind with a teeming world of legendary beings!

Yes, legends, too – especially those that come from the distant past, from the childhood of mankind – parade before us people with evocative names, rich in poetry. Ulysses, Oedipus, Moses, the Buddha, Orpheus and Parsifal are archetypes for ever inscribed on the human mind. All the gods of mythology are there within us, embodying from our earliest childhood the various aspects of our destiny.

And also in our most vivid dreams, when we are asleep, the characters sometimes have strange names which make us wonder where we could have taken them from. We sense the importance of finding out the meaning of such names, so clearly imprinted on our memory. Often we have no success, and that is irritating, for we feel that the essential message of the dream is eluding us. But if some unexpected association of ideas puts us on the track, and gives us the key to the dream, we wonder at the ingenious nature of this 'dream-work' as Freud called it, which so cleverly conceals its meaning.

In dreams as well as in legends there appear also at times magic phrases or formulas, solemnly and often repeatedly uttered, the importance of which as clues to the meaning of the dream one senses. They do not belong to any known language, these strings of words, but they have not been chosen at random. They are always significant, but their meaning is veiled.

But let us return to the child. As we have said, it is through his name that he becomes aware that he is a person, a unique being. He alone answers to that name, is called upon to answer; and it is what awakens in him the feeling of his personal identity and his personal responsibility. In the infant classes he is still known by his first name, at the age when this awakening personal awareness comes. He will find to his surprise that further up the school he will be known by his surname, a change which marks his promotion into a more ceremonious and conventional society.

He may of course suffer the same misadventure as did the little Alain I mentioned at the beginning: he may meet other children with the same Christian name.

Frequently, even – first names go very much by fashion. Parents who think they have found an original name for their child often find when he gets to school that the name has become quite common. As the story of the two Alains showed, the child has a proprietary feeling about his Christian name which society instinctively respects.

There are classes, and even clubs, in which the difficulty is got over by the addition of a number: Alain I, Alain II and so on. This is less formal than adding the surname, as is usually done in society at large. Thus popes and kings, whose surnames are forgotten, are also distinguished by numbers.

Children, however, are often given nicknames which become a quite personal possession of their own. Not all children have nicknames. One may wonder why some do. No doubt it is sometimes in order to distinguish them from others of the same name. Occasionally, too, they are given spontaneously and without malice because of some physical characteristic such as red hair, exceptional stature or agility. It was for this reason that in my secondary school they called me 'Rubber-legs'. That was the first social success of my shy and inhibited orphan's childhood.

A success, did I call it? Yes, it seems to me that the children who receive a nickname are mostly those who stand out from the anonymous mass of their fellows, either as leaders or as duffers. The nickname is a sort of tribute given by impersonal society to the person, to those among its members who are more personal. It is a sign of a popularity which may be either flattering or scornful. A school class acts in accordance with a primitive, gregarious and brutal crowd psychology, occasionally encouraged by a teacher who uses laughter at the expense of an abnormal and defenceless pupil as a means of welding the others together under his own control. It is a pitiless age, as La Fontaine remarked.

Some nicknames are laudatory; others are the expression of an innocent sense of humour; yet others are cruel and spiteful, and can do irreparable harm. Whereas Christian names are carefully chosen by parents, nicknames usually arise spontaneously. Even if they are born of the quick wit of a single person, they have to gain acceptance by the crowd. I once belonged to a student club in which each initiate received a nickname which was intended to be taken into common use. But most of them fell at once into disuse, no doubt simply because they were artificial.

Furthermore, while the nickname has an influence on the person, there is also the influence that the person has on the nickname, which may in this way be exorcized. When a man is likeable, his friends may continue calling him by a grotesque nickname without feeling it to be grotesque any more, since the name loses its literal sense in order to designate solely the respected person. The reversal may be complete. In Marcel Pagnol's comedy *Topaze*,[6] the character who receives this ridiculous nickname – a character created by Fernandel in the film version – from being the butt of the crowd changes his hearers' views by improvising a witty song on his nickname, and getting the laughter on to his side.

There are also family nicknames which are charming while the child is tiny, but ridiculous when he grows bigger. Sometimes, of course, this persistence of the childish nickname may signify that the person concerned has remained infantile, or it may mean that those about him are refusing to recognize his right to become an adult. In any case the nickname is bound up with the destiny of the person, either influencing it or expressing it. It may also be personal and selective in a different sense — not in relation to the one who receives it, but in relation to the one who gives it. The mother, a brother, a friend, gives the child a nickname which no one else uses, and this marks the existence of a particular emotional bond. Similarly, between husband and wife nicknames are common and are full of affectionate meaning.

These points concerning nicknames apply also to Christian names, their repercussions being much greater owing to the fact that the Christian name is deliberately chosen by the parents. Some of these names too are ridiculous. I shall refrain from giving examples so as not to hurt anyone's feelings. But every reader will have come across them. Such names can do serious harm to a child, beginning with teasing by schoolmates, to which the child is particularly sensitive. While mockery can give rise to a scornful nickname, a given-name that is too fanciful, unusual, or absurd, can give rise to mockery. But now the sufferer knows whom to blame.

Of course you may point out to me that most children have several given-names inscribed on their birth certificates. There are people, in America especially, who make their signatures with two or three Christian names. Perhaps without realizing it they do so because it sounds grander. Princes receive a large number of given-names as a sign of their elevated rank. When it is merely to avoid confusion with possible namesakes, it is usual to confine oneself to indicating the initials of the secondary names. Sometimes I find myself wondering what the name is when I am told only the initial letter.

Most people, therefore, could, if they did not like their ordinary Christian name, adopt another of their official names. The surprising thing is that this is very rare, even among those who claim to have suffered all their lives from bearing a name they thought ridiculous, ugly or cumbersome. It seems, therefore, as if the usual name received from one's parents has a sacred character. It has some sort of magic power, so that one may fear or even hate it, but not dare to do anything about it.

. As I have already pointed out, I believe that this derives from the part played by the given-name in the personal identity of its bearer. And so to change one's name is to break one's continuity as a person, to cut oneself off from the whole of one's past, which has defined one's person up to that point.

Proof of this is the fact that a change of name may be desired by an individual and accepted by society when the change has a religious significance. The new name asserts that a new life is beginning, like a new birth, by divine election. The Bible provides many examples of this: Abram becomes Abraham, Jacob takes the name of Israel, Saul of Tarsus becomes Paul, and Jesus gives

Simon the name of Peter (the Rock), to indicate that he is to be the foundation of his church. It is worth noting that after Peter's denial and before Jesus had rehabilitated him with the command 'Feed my sheep', Jesus addressed him by his old name: 'Simon, son of John, do you love me more than these?' (John 21.15).

By analogy, Catholic monks and nuns choose a new name when they take their monastic vows. This is yet another sign of the identity of the name and the person: for a new person, a new name. But it is only an analogy, and in the protestant community of Taizé the brothers retain their baptismal names, names which already indicate the new birth of the Christian.

Quite different are the pseudonyms adopted by writers and actors, by spies and undercover agents. The similarity need not surprise us. Georges Gusdorf says[7] that the reason why Voltaire wrote under a number of different pseudonyms was so as to escape the Bastille. It was thus a pretext. But he goes on to say that Voltaire was no doubt giving way to an inclination to reveal himself as a multiple personality, playing a number of different roles, 'a crowd which he created so that he could become lost in it'. The pseudonym therefore hardly raises the problem of identity any more than the conventional disguises and fancy dress worn in a carnival.

On the other hand, society demands strict adherence to a complicated procedure if a name is to be changed simply for personal convenience. It recognizes and sanctions in this way the right of parents to choose their child's Christian name. In Switzerland, even 'the trans-

lation of a French or Italian forename into German, or
vice versa, subsequent to the registration of the forename,
is prohibited'. This interdiction upon the translation of
Christian names results from 'the immutability of the
name to which a person has a right'. It will be noted that
it is not so much a right of the person concerned as a
denial of his right to change his given-name, and the confirmation of his parents' right to give him an immutable
name.

I have culled the above quotations from a booklet published by the Swiss Association of Registrars, which
regulates their conduct and that of the parents in this
matter in my country. It contains a list of the 3,761 forenames in use in Switzerland in our four national languages: 1,058 German, 742 French, 1,176 Italian and 785
Romansh. It will be seen that Italian has the record for
imagination. The authors do not claim that their list is
exhaustive. It is strictly limited, so as to protect children
against possible extravagances on the part of their
parents: 'In choosing a name, parents should take particular care that their child will not find himself obliged
when he grows up to bear a name which will lower him
or make him look ridiculous in the eyes of society. This
consideration should take precedence over a desire to
commemorate certain biblical, historical or legendary
personages, cinema stars or individuals mentioned in
popular songs of the day!'

In Geneva, as in other areas touched by the Reforma-
tion, Old Testament names used to be especially favoured.
A friend of mine called Isaac, who lived abroad, used his

second Christian name, Charles, to avoid being thought Jewish. The reader will have noticed, of course, that the tone of the registrars' booklet is that of recommendation rather than command. 'The registrar,' it points out, 'ought to advise parents and seek to dissuade them when they wish to give their child an unsuitable forename.' Clearly this note of caution shows the concern of the authorities not to be suspected of encroaching in an authoritarian fashion upon parents' rights.

These rights are in fact unequivocally asserted: 'The determining factors are, first, the wish of the father; and failing this, that of the mother.' There are some exceptions, however. Simone de Beauvoir informs us[8] that among certain primitive peoples it is the oldest members of the tribe who choose names for the new-born. This is still no more than a variation of the hierarchy of generations, which puts back the parents' prerogative into the hands of the grandparents.

It could be put further back still! In exceptional circumstances God reserves to himself the choice of a name, and imposes it as a mark that the child who is to bear it is predestined to his service, even before he is conceived in the womb. Thus, when the angel of the Lord appears to old Zechariah in the Temple, he says to him, 'Your wife Elizabeth is to bear you a son and you must name him John' (Luke 1.13). So parents may be divinely inspired in their choice of a name for their child. Even so they are obliged to obey this inspiration, as Zechariah did.

In the emotion caused by his vision Zechariah had lost

the power of speech. And so, at the child's circumcision, it is Elizabeth who declares, 'He is to be called John.' Their relations are astonished at the unusual choice, and turn to question Zechariah, who writes on a tablet, 'His name is John.' At once the father recovers the power of speech and praises God. One detail is particularly interesting – the reason why the family is surprised at the choice of the name of John is that 'no one in the family has that name'. That indicates that John the Baptist will detach himself from his clan, from the family tradition, and will mark the personal intervention of God in the history of the world.

In the same way, when the angel Gabriel appears to the Virgin Mary, he says to her, 'You are to conceive and bear a son, and you must name him Jesus' (Luke 1.31). Obviously the Bible attaches great importance to the choice of the personal name, and to its religious significance. Apart from these exceptional cases which I have just mentioned, God has delegated to the parents the right to choose a name for their child.

This is expressed by the church in the sacrament of baptism. Baptism, as I have pointed out, is the religious symbol of the new birth of the Christian, and of the fact that the child belongs to God. At the same time it is a solemn proclamation in public of the baptismal name chosen by the parents. Depending on the denomination, rite or theological belief to which the parents adhere, baptism may take place in infancy or else later, at an age when the child is capable of making a decision for himself.

But the baptismal naming is always no more than a consecration of the name already decided upon by the parents even before the birth of the child. The giving of the name comes first, and is itself, whether or not the parents look upon it as such, a religious act. In baptism God himself, and the officiant who personifies him, respectfully adopt the name chosen by the parents.

In this book I should like to lead parents to a better understanding of the meaning of this right which God has accorded to them of giving their child his Christian name, the name which confers on him his dignity as a person. That shows us that God calls on man to share in his creative work, not only in natural procreation, but also in the creation of the spiritual world, of this world of persons which is the people of God.

The fact that there is a connection between speech and creation is seen right from the opening verses of the Bible: 'God said, "Let there be light", and there was light' (Gen. 1.3). Moreover, God at once gives names to his creation: 'God called light "day", and darkness he called "night".' You will notice that there is a slight difference in meaning in the new names, compared with the old: the differentiation between light and darkness is static, whereas the alternation of day and night is dynamic, and signifies the introduction of time, of becoming, into creation. Thus the significance of the 'days' of creation is its long development in time, which accords so well with the views of science.

Only creatures have names; the Creator has none. Mankind has attributed many names to him, but he has none at all, for it is impossible to confine him within a definition or a limited image. The biblical writers carefully avoided giving him a name. The Hebrew tetragram which is translated as Yahweh in our scriptures 'is in fact not a name,' Georges Gusdorf tells us,[9] 'but an affirmation of existence, a verbal form signifying "he is"'. Jesus himself calls God quite simply 'the Father'.

But God has associated man with his creative activity. He created him in his own image, and then charged him to give names to the beasts of the earth and the birds of the air. Again, Georges Gusdorf expresses this in a striking phrase: 'To name is to call into existence.'[10]

The priest–doctor Marc Oraison[11] puts it in his own individual way: 'One day a man and a woman met . . . Some time later, in a corner of a hollow muscle inside my mother, a particular assemblage of cells and molecules began to develop, parasitically . . . Before long, they noticed it. And they said, "If it's a boy, he will be called Marc." There you are! I already exist, I am already named, I answer in advance to a particular idea of me that someone has . . . But I do not know it; I shall only know it much later on . . . There I am, existing without knowing it . . . I am travelling on the journey between my blastula stage and my death . . . And I can explore nothing of either . . .'

The Book of Genesis further states that each creature 'was to bear the name the man would give it' (Gen. 2.19). We can see in this passage the biblical foundation of science, since all science is never anything more than a language. But we may also see in it the creation of con-

25

sciousness: the animals were already in existence, by nature, beforehand, but in charging man with the task of giving them names God causes him to become conscious of their existence. The French psychoanalyst Mme. Levy-Valensi [12] has brought out the importance of this function entrusted by God to man.

So the sacred right of parents to give their child the name that will make him a person is recognized. The child does not only inherit his family name, marking his place in the paternal lineage, but also has his given-name, which is much more personal to him. When a woman changes her name on marriage she retains the forename she received from her parents. Physical resemblances confirm this line of dependence — resemblances which play such a large part in the conversations that take place around the cradle: 'Isn't he like his mother!' — 'I think he's the very image of his father!'

All this is expressed in the right of parents to choose the name. It is not only respected by the registrar of births and by the clergyman who officiates at the baptism. It is written in the human heart. This is true in the Bible, since even in the case of John the Baptist and in that of Jesus, to which I have referred, the parents still freely chose the name inspired in them by God.

The fact that parents have this right has, I think, an even deeper significance. It symbolizes in fact the dependence of children upon their parents, a dependence from which they can never escape despite all the rebellions and rejections that may be in store for them. No doubt there are some of my readers who will protest in their hearts against what I have just said. They will think that I am siding with the parents even when they are unworthy of the authority they claim to exercise. I have been the recipient of too many confidences not to recognize that there are rebellions and rejections which are legitimate and salutary.

Nevertheless, to rebel against someone is still to take account of him, to do him the honour of making him a target, to take up a position with reference to him. Whether you imitate your father, conform with him and his desires, or whether you contradict him and oppose his wishes, you are still acting with reference to him. It is as if every man retained for ever a certain responsibility towards his parents, even when they are unworthy of it. All the more so when they do merit it, of course. It is as if every man considering his own life had to answer to his parents for it, whether or not they are still living, and say to them, 'This is what I have done with the name you gave me.' I am reminded of Goethe's profound comment, 'What you have received from your forefathers, acquire it so as to possess it.'

To make a name for oneself is to confer in one's own person a certain honour, a certain authority or notoriety, on the name one has received from one's parents, and no one, however humble he may be, is free of that ambition. Here again there is still a certain reference to the person of the parents. The French actor-playwright Sacha Guitry is well known for his wit. His father, Lucien Guitry, was also a famous actor, who had created with notable success the role of Edmond Rostand's Chantecler.

And so the son, Sacha, wrote: 'I already had a name; I had to make a forename for myself.'

I found myself in a somewhat similar situation. My father was a well-known and respected figure in Geneva, famous as a preacher. He was also a poet, and had received, unsolicited, a literary prize. One day a close friend of mine, a psychoanalyst, asked me, 'Have you ever thought of becoming a pastor like your father?' 'No,' I replied, 'the idea has never entered my mind.' 'Then one might think,' he went on, 'that you had a very ambivalent attitude to your father – you venerated him and wanted to follow in his footsteps, but would not let yourself compete with him by becoming a second Pastor Tournier. Your subconscious would seem to have found a happy solution to the dilemma, in that you have become a pastor for many of us without having the formal title, and using medicine instead of theology.'

I felt at once that my friend was right. My father died two months after I was born. But his shadowy figure has none the less hovered over my whole life – as it still does. It seems to me that the Freudians, interested as they are in the Oedipus complex, have little to say about the situation of the boy whose father has died. Perhaps it is because that has less effect on his development than might be expected. Certainly I never had to assert myself, as others have to, against my father. One does not have conflicts with a person who is dead. But at a deeper level I was nevertheless shaped by my relationship with him. Thinking it over, there was one detail that caught my attention: when I was young I did not sign myself with my Christian name in full, but only with an initial, as some do. The day came when without thinking about it I started to sign with my full Christian name. Now it seems to me that the change came at the time when I dared to take my place in the world, whereas until then, lacking the support that a father represents, I had been shyly making myself as inconspicuous as possible, by hiding something of myself.

However that may be, the Christian name which my parents gave me is a sort of seal placed upon me, which I still bear after they are dead and gone. If I had ever had the honour of meeting Pope Paul VI, I should have been able respectfully to say to him that apart from our common Christian faith I have a special link with him, in that we bear the same Christian name, doubtless for the same reason: he chose it in reference to St Paul, the great missionary. And it was certainly on the same ground that my parents chose it for me.

The reader will see in what sense I speak of the name as a sign of a dependence upon the parents which is never effaced, whether or not they are worthy of it. It marks an intention on the part of the parents, declared even before the child's birth, in virtue of a right which is neither formal nor moral, but quite natural.

I recall the discussions that Nelly and I had when she was expecting our first child. The ambivalence in regard to my father was already at work without my realizing it. We wanted to retain the memory of my father, Louis Tournier, in the name we gave to our child; but we did not want to give him precisely the same name, for fear

29

such a well-known name might be a burden to the child. So we called him Jean-Louis, a name that is very common in the neighbouring canton of Vaud, where both my mother and my wife came from.

2

The Problem of
Possessiveness

There always remain some traces of the dependence of the child upon his parents. While the child is still quite small this dependence is obvious and almost complete. All parents the world over enjoy being like gods for their children in this way, playing the role of Providence for them. But if as the child grows this dependence does not diminish, it becomes an obstacle to his personal development, preventing him from becoming a person distinct from his parents, acquiring his own individual tastes, aspirations and beliefs.

Sometimes parents instinctively try in good faith to keep their children in a state of dependence upon them, either by suggestion, or by emotional blackmail, or else by using their authority and insisting upon obedience. The child is theirs, they have rights over him because he belongs to them. Such parents are termed possessive. The very parents who have conferred upon their child the dignity of being a person by giving him his name, fail to treat him as a person when later on they look upon him as a thing to be possessed.

These two apparently contradictory tendencies go together: in the right of parents to give the name, we see the germ of the feeling of ownership which can give rise to grave problems. This is another example of the association of the ideas of naming and possessing to which I have already referred in quoting Georges Gusdorf and Jean Piaget on the subject of primitive peoples and children. Dr Jacques Sarano writes[1] similarly: 'To name is to possess, to make sure of one's hold over a person.' Before you lend a book you are careful to write your name in it, so that the borrower will be in no doubt that it is your property. Conversely, to name oneself is to deliver oneself into someone else's hands. That is why groups such as the Samaritans guarantee the anonymity of those who telephone them in desperation. On that condition the caller can impart the most intimate confidences without feeling he is 'giving himself away'.

It is because I have seen so many tragic victims of parental possessiveness that I decided to write this book on the subject of the person of the child. It is, after all, the respect due to the child as a person which can open parents' eyes and stop them giving way to their instinctive reflex of possessiveness. So I have it at heart to explain now with care what I think on this subject.

A first remark: the anti-abortionists also invoke respect for the person of the child. Of course I agree with them. All abortion is murder. Nevertheless the law does not forbid all crimes. Some it even ordains – in war, for example. It is the role of the law, therefore, to define which crimes are punishable and which are not.

But in the polemics about legal abortion it is respect for life that is referred to rather than respect for the person.

The respect for the person of the child that I am talking about here is not only respect for his life, but respect for his right to be himself, to realize himself in his own way and not in accordance with the ideas, principles, tastes, ambitions and dreams of his parents. The child feels this very early, well before the conflicts of adolescence, in particular at about the age of four, in the phase that has been called the age of opposition. All he can do to assert himself is to say 'No': 'Come here!' – 'No!' – 'Be quiet!' – 'No!' – 'Say good morning!' – 'No!'

The parents' reaction will be decisive. Of course I am not saying that they must give way to the child's every whim. But they must recognize the limits of their own whims, and in particular they must avoid all those commands and threats that have no other aim than to test out the child's docility, to break his will and force him to capitulate. What is it, then, which marks the proper limit of the rights of parents? It is this very realization that the child is not a toy but a person to be respected.

Instinctively, parents the world over see their children as pretty toys, gifts from heaven, which like all toys are meant for the pleasure that playing with them affords. Couples seeking to adopt a child usually ask for one that is still quite tiny. Their hope is that he will the more easily become attached to his adoptive parents. But no doubt it is also sometimes in order to have the pleasure of playing with him as if he were a doll.

But the word 'toy' has another significance: not the

innocent pleasure of the plaything, but the pleasure of domineering, of manoeuvring another person as one wills, toying with him, exploiting his weakness and using him. All social life, all human relationships, are a game. But each of us feels a certain resentment when he realizes that he is no longer an equal and respected partner in the game, but has become a mere plaything in someone else's hands. It makes no difference whether it is as a child, a wife, a voter, a worker, or a customer − the injury is the same. Consider how frightened hospital patients are of being used as guinea-pigs. Each of us feels in his heart that the proper limit is respect for other people as persons.

So, you parents, it is this respect for the person of your child that defines the limit of your rights. It is no abstract legalistic limitation, but a quite practical living one. If you disregard it you will be punished not by some avenging authority, but by the spontaneous deterioration of your relationship with your child.

Here is an example. The name you choose for him, either lightly or very seriously, is chosen by you − such is your right − in accordance with your own good pleasure, and he will have to carry it about with him all his life, whether he likes it or not. Naturally you have no means of knowing whether he will like it when he is old enough to have his own personal tastes. Whether his likes and dislikes will coincide or not with your own will depend on the spirit in which you bring him up − on whether it is a spirit imbued with respect for him as a person or a spirit of possessiveness.

In fact, our affectivity is stronger with persons than with things, so that we generally find that where children have a happy affective relationship with their parents they like the name they have been given, and vice versa. In other words, the child will like his name, and will generally adhere quite naturally to his parents' choice, just as he will also accept their orders, their advice, or their reprimands, if he feels that they are bringing him up for his own sake and not for theirs, if their conduct towards him is dictated by a desire to help him to become himself and not by a wish to get from him all the satisfaction they can.

I have said that this is 'generally' the case, because psychological determinisms of this sort do not have the same sort of mathematical rigour as do the laws of physics. A man may dislike his Christian name for purely aesthetic reasons that are not susceptible of psychological analysis. This may also be a sign that he does not like himself, since the name is so closely identified with the person. See, for instance, how the lover dotes on the Christian name of the girl he loves. He makes little tunes of it to himself, or writes it all over the margins of his exercise books.

This does not mean that I do not sometimes ask those who consult me, both those who are well and those who are ill, whether they like their forenames. If they reply that they do not, then I am on the alert, like a setter that scents the game it seeks. I shall listen with special care when such a person is talking to me about his childhood and his relationship with his parents. Quite possibly he will tell me they were splendid people; it is quite possible for a docile child to have solicitous parents who decide everything for him and spare him any effort at making personal judgments for himself. And in fact it is his person which remains undeveloped in such a case, and he is left in an impersonal state, entirely conditioned by his parents. And so his shyness and lack of self-confidence bring him to me.

Unfortunately, however, there are much more tragic cases, in which the person has really been crushed. Often the child has been aware from a very early age of a lack of ease in his relationship with his parents, without being able to discern its cause. It does not always mean that he has not been loved! But instead of enjoying his parents' love and blossoming in its warmth, he has had to fight against being suffocated by it. Even with normal parents the emancipation of the child is not accomplished without conflict. Even Jesus, at the age of twelve, had to defend himself against his parents' reproaches because instead of docilely following them he had busied himself with preparing for his own future by staying behind in Jerusalem among the theologians. You will recall with what firmness he spoke to them then.

But possessive parents will not tolerate such resistance, and they break it. The tragic thing is that they often appeal to morality in support of their point of view. They invoke the respect due to parents, and even biblical texts such as St Paul's words, 'Children, be obedient to your parents' (Eph. 6.1, 4), without noticing that the apostle then goes on to say, 'And parents, never drive your children to resentment.' A vicious circle is set up: the more the child resists, the more afraid do the parents become of losing him, and consequently the more possessive and jealous. They combat and forbid the friendships which the child forms outside the family, they impose their likes and prejudices upon him in his activities, his games, his studies, his dress, and even his hair-style.

Above all they inculcate in him an attitude of submission, and the notion that his first duty in life is not to upset his parents. In such situations I always think of Dr Arnold Stocker's words: 'Neurosis results from an inner conflict between a correct intuition and a false suggestion.' [2]

The correct intuition of the child is that he is a person, distinct from his parents; and that he must assert and defend himself, gradually assuming responsibility for himself, listening to his inner voice so as to construct his individual life in accordance with his own tastes, convictions and ambitions; that he has as much right as other people to pleasures and satisfactions. The false suggestion inculcated in him by his parents is that he owes everything to them, that he must forget himself in order to devote himself to others – and especially to them, obeying them in all things, never opposing them, since they have so many other things to worry about that any manifestation of his own personal will can only be selfish! In short, that the parents are always right, as one of the first psychoanalysts, Allendy, so justly pointed out.[3]

I am not exaggerating this picture. I have seen it only too often. Literature knows it too, in the person of

Cinderella, whose very pleasures can only be an ephemeral dream. These Cinderellas, heroes of unmarked devotion, continue to be exploited by everyone all their lives, with no one paying any attention to them as persons. As persons they have been trampled upon. They come to doubt their own existence, to feel they exist only in the services they perform, to have no idea what they want in life, except for dreams that have no more reality than fairy-tales.

This 'possessive deviation' is more frequent in the mother, though I think it unfair that people only ever talk of maternal possessiveness, as if there were not also possessive fathers as well. But the latter usually operate more crudely. They dominate through the fear they inspire and the authority of their commands. Men aspire more to command, and women to possess. A woman dominates by her very love, by the emotional ascendancy that she establishes. Sometimes she goes as far as threatening or attempting to kill herself, and terrifies the child. Moreover, even in these extreme cases, the father tends to aid and abet the mother by urging submission so as to spare himself unpleasant scenes, with the result that a child feels bereft of paternal protection. Sometimes the father bears a special responsibility for the situation, in that the mother is seeking compensation for her own disappointment in marriage in the domination and influence she exerts over her child.

A daughter may be used as a consolation for a mother's disappointment with her other children. The others may be less credulous, and know how to defend themselves against her possessiveness. They manage to free themselves at an early stage from their mother's apron-strings. The mother lets them go, and makes up for their defection by praising her little Cinderella as her faithful friend, while at the same time endlessly directing at her the criticisms she does not dare to make of the others.

What a joy it is sometimes to be able to play just a little of the part of the fairy godmother by reviving the person of some Cinderella that has been crushed since childhood. They remind me of those Japanese flowers or dolls that look like small tightly compressed balls of paper until they are immersed in water, when they gradually expand and turn into delicate flowers with brightly coloured petals, or graceful figurines in rich kimonos, with long pins in their hair and tiny parasols. The American Carl Rogers writes of the joy of the psychotherapist who feels he is 'witnessing the birth of a person'.[4] But while all one has to do with the Japanese compressed paper models is to put them in water, great patience is required in awakening the sleeping personality. What it has to be immersed in is a personal relationship, in which the individual who has been valued only for his usefulness to others feels that he is accepted for what he is, as a person in his own right.

The decisive thing in the development of the person is the personal relationship. It is important not to confuse the problem of possessiveness with that of severity or indulgence. Parents may be either severe or indulgent, and still be possessive. I am not saying that the kind of upbringing – authoritarian or liberal – is a matter of no importance, but each always has advantages and dis-advantages which must be carefully weighed.

Nevertheless what weighs most heavily, what is really harmful, is possessiveness. This is not one more educational theory to be debated. It is a matter of the fundamental attitude of the parents towards the child – whether they look upon him as a person, or on the contrary as an object which can be disposed of like a piece of property. 'Each of our children,' writes Dr William Brunat, 'has a right to the implicit and total recognition of his human personality. Let us agree, even in the case of the infant, to respect his dignity as a person – we cannot look upon heredity as if it were a title to property.'[5]

Possessiveness is almost always unconscious. Suggest to these parents that they are being possessive, and they will protest with the utmost energy and sincerity. They love the child so much, they are thinking only of him and his future, for his own good. They want him to grow up to be an exemplary adult, and so they are inculcating right principles in him, a proper family spirit, unselfishness and consideration for others. They want him to be their friend, and will not tolerate that he should hide anything from them. And if the child expresses an opinion they consider to be bad, or a desire they judge to be harmful, they think it their duty to fight against such pernicious tendencies. They are so hurt by any conflict with him, that they only find peace when he conforms with their correct opinions.

In a shop the daughter always chooses a dress that is too

long or too short, too showy or too dull, too ordinary or too eccentric. The mother knows better than her daughter what is right for her; she must train her taste. Or else the mother is so fond of pink that she cannot conceive of her daughter not liking it. Nor does the girl know how to choose her friends. Why should her mother let her form an attachment to some badly brought-up person who will have a deplorable influence upon her? She must be protected from bad company. Her health, too, must be safeguarded, and so the mother considers it her duty to watch over her like a broody hen, dressing her in clothes that are too warm, and forbidding her to go out in the evening.

The reader will see how difficult it is to know when one is being possessive. In fact love always has something of possessiveness in it. One sees it in the lover who says he cannot live without the girl he loves, or bear to let her go. He fights to win her back, to possess her. Between parents and children a certain amount of possessiveness on each side is normal and necessary. Children whose parents are not sufficiently possessive feel that they are not loved. We all oscillate, in regard to all those we love, between too much and too little possessiveness, without really being aware of it.

The more you love a child, the more you identify with him, and the more you expect him to identify with you, and also the more danger are you in of being annoyed if he acts differently from the way you want him to. Only rarely do we have flashes of insight when we realize that we are not acting from love but from possessiveness. I shall always remember one such moment, when I had just tweaked my son's ear, and I realized all at once that I had done so more violently than was proper for such a small child. I was very upset. Who is there who can boast that he has never abused his physical or moral power over a child?

The child too is possessive towards his parents, his grandparents, or his teachers. Listen to the tone of voice in which a little girl says 'my daddy': in the same way as her daddy says 'my daughter', a wife says 'my husband', and a husband 'my wife'. A few days ago our grandsons were playing with some little girls who live near by. One of the girls referred to my wife, as the boys do, as 'grandma'. Our grandsons at once protested, 'You've no right to call her "grandma"! She's not yours, she's ours!'

Thence comes the eternal ambiguity of love – of friendship even! Which of you has not sometimes had to hold off from an over-possessive friend, to refuse to go on a holiday with him, perhaps, because his passionate and demanding friendship weighs too heavily on you, hamstrings you, because he does not respect you as a person but tries to turn you into a thing to be possessed.

This is just the paradox I described in the matter of choosing a name: by calling the child Francis while still carrying him in her womb, the mother is already conferring upon him his dignity as a person; but in the keenness of her love she is already also saying 'my Francis, my treasure'. And possessiveness, which ignores the person, has already come into it, like the tender coming behind the locomotive. Possessiveness feeds the fire of love as the coal from the tender feeds the furnace of the engine.

I shall be told that habits have changed, that the young of today know how to defend themselves against the possessiveness of parents, even long before adolescence, that they very often misuse the independence they have been able to win. After reading the pages I have just written, some of my readers may be thinking that my age is beginning to show, that I belong to a past age, that I am describing the relationship between parents and children as it may well have been once, but is no longer. And it is true that the victims of possessive parents whose confidences I listen to today are inclined to be jealous of young people who are able to assert themselves nowadays in a way that they themselves were not able to in the past.

But have young people become more persons, that is to say responsible individuals enjoying inner freedom? I am not at all sure. They conform to the customs of their age as those of a past era did to theirs, but the real problem of possessiveness has not been resolved. There have always been two possible reactions to the constraint of possessiveness: submission or rebellion. Some children of possessive parents submit, others break free. It is a matter of the relative strengths of parent and child.

Moreover, looking more closely into the problem one finds that there is a third reaction, worse than either of the others, a paradoxical mixture of submission and rebellion. Complete submission and determined escape are two relatively healthy reactions, because they are clear and straightforward. Thus the child who capitulates to his mother's possessiveness is blocked in his personal development, but does not realize it. He scarcely suffers any sense of frustration, and often sings the praises of the exemplary love of the mother he adores. This adoration is precisely what possessive parents seek.

So we must not confuse possessiveness with authoritarian domination. It is often through her inexhaustible love, her limitless devotion, her kindness, her gentleness and her services that a mother binds sons or daughters to herself, and turns them into slaves at the same time as spoiling them. She makes herself indispensable, and so arms herself against the danger of seeing them break away. And if the day comes when the child realizes how dependent he has become, he experiences that mixture of revolt and submission, and suffers more acutely as a result. He is ambivalent, as the psychologists say. He would like to free himself, but he cannot, and he blames himself for not daring to do so, so successfully has the mother persuaded him by her love that he cannot live without her.

It would therefore be naive to imagine that possessiveness has been exorcized because a change of habits has shaken the traditional authority of parents. If nowadays many parents give way to their children's claim to independence, it is not so much out of respect for them as persons, as because times have changed, and the young can now assert themselves in a way they could not do in the past. Parents are bowing to the inevitable, even though it goes against the grain. Their true feelings come out in their criticisms of the young. It is possible to compromise grudgingly, hiding or repressing one's possessive-ness without being freed from it.

Possessiveness does not depend on custom. Its roots are too deep in the human heart. So far I have dealt only with its harmful effects in blocking the development of children. It can last a whole lifetime. We all know how a daughter-in-law can suffer at the hands of a mother-in-law who is possessive about her son. Here again, the mother is quite unaware that she is being possessive. It is she who accuses her daughter-in-law of being possessive and of trying to take her beloved son away from her.

Grandparents, too, often suffer because they do not see enough of their grandchildren, and complain that the parents are too possessive. Many a single woman suffers because she only rarely sees her nephews and nieces, or even her married brother, putting it down to jealousy on the part of her sister-in-law. The striking thing about all these conflicts, the thing that proves that they are due to unconscious factors, is that they abound in the most cultured families, among eminent people, philosophers, psychologists, marriage counsellors, and among religious people who most sincerely profess the primacy of love and self-denial.

Consequently we must ask ourselves whether there can be any answer to this curse of possessiveness, the source of so many conflicts and so much oppression among the very people who are most closely bound by the bonds of love. Thus a mother's love is often cited as the model of disinterested love, calling forth the noblest devotion and sacrifice. And it is true. But it is also, through a strange and unconscious distortion, maternal love which can weigh down upon a child and reduce him to slavery. Psychologists have spoken of the 'devouring mother', and have shown that she figures as an archetype in the oldest legends of the human race.

One can embrace the object of one's love so strongly, so strongly that one crushes him to death. Hate can kill, we all know. Policemen were invented to curb its murderous effects. But love also can kill, and there are no policemen who can deal with that. In the same way patriotism can appear to be a most disinterested form of love, the source of exemplary sacrifices. We Swiss children were taught that in our history lessons at school, when we heard about the heroic wars of independence which laid the foundations of our country. But how many, many crimes have been committed in the name of patriotism!

You see the extreme importance of this problem of the relation between love and possessiveness. It is an everyday problem, not only between parents and children, but also between social classes and sovereign states. It is not just a question of dominating when one is strong enough, or of giving in when one is no longer so. It is a matter of our personal attitude towards other people: whether we respect them as persons or not. To manipulate a person in accordance with our own desires is to fail in this respect; but to abdicate one's responsibility towards him is also to fail. To young people capitulation of this kind can feel like abandonment.

So we can neither give way to the instinct of possession,

nor love with a love that is exempt from it. The question is a disturbing one, going far beyond the limits of the subject of this book. But we are trying here to understand it in essence, rather as the chemist in the laboratory brings about in his little test-tube a reaction which will later be put into operation in the factory on an industrial scale.

What we see is that right from the start the purest love and the most dangerous possessiveness are inextricably bound up together: love, the essential creative force, and possessiveness, equally essentially destructive. Perhaps some of my readers have been thinking that it is all a matter of degree, that we need to be sufficiently possessive, but not too much so. But they will also have felt, as I do, that this is a most unsatisfactory answer to the problem. It shifts into the sphere of quantity a problem which is essentially one of quality – the quality of our love for others. 'What is decisive,' writes Martin Buber,[6] 'is the not-being-an-object.'

I think the only valid answer was given by St Paul. I give here only two brief quotations, whereas one ought to reread all his letters, which illustrate in a thousand ways that quality of life which Jesus brings to the heart of the Christian, making it possible for him to detach himself without abdicating, to be disinterested but not indifferent, to possess as if not possessing.

It is subtle, of course, but it is manifestly one of the great psychological messages of the gospel. It is worth pausing over this. St Paul writes: 'Those who have wives should live as though they had none; and those who mourn should live as though they had nothing to mourn for; those who are enjoying life should live as though they had nothing to laugh about; those whose life is buying things should live as though they had nothing of their own; and those who have to deal with the world should not become engrossed in it' (I Cor. 7.29). Elsewhere, after recalling all the tribulations and persecutions he has undergone, he exclaims, '[We are] thought most miserable and yet we are always rejoicing; taken for paupers though we make others rich, for people having nothing though we have everything' (II Cor. 6.10).

Yes, to possess as if not possessing. Such is the great message of the Bible. Man can never truly possess anything. He is but the steward of the goods that God entrusts to him, for 'the earth and everything that is in it belong to the Lord' (I Cor. 10.26). This is true of all material riches, of money, of the means of production, even of the land we own, the redistribution of which every forty-nine years was prescribed by the law of Moses, in order to restore their patrimony to families that had had to sell it owing to straitened financial circumstances. Such is the principle laid down by the Bible for economic life, although no Christian state dares to implement it, nor any so-called Christian political party to propose it.

And if this is true of material goods, it is much more so in the case of persons: 'To Yahweh belong earth and all it holds, the world and all who live in it' (Ps. 24.1). Every person belongs to God; no man may exercise a right of possession over another. If it took many centuries for people to realize that slavery was incompatible with Christianity, and then that the worker could not be likened to a commodity to be bought and sold, it will no doubt also take time for it to be seen that the right of parents over their children, as it is still conceived, comes very near to slavery. Figures have lately been published in Britain showing that 700 children die every year in the United Kingdom as a consequence of maltreatment by their parents. No one can doubt that the same is true in Switzerland and in all civilized countries. Doctors, who know what goes on inside families, know it to be so.

If men and women are only the stewards of the material goods which God lends them, they are all the more so of the children God entrusts to them. 'Children belong to God before they belong to their parents,' wrote Dr Vittoz.[7] The right to give the child his name, of which we have spoken, can be seen in this light to be delegated from God, and implies the responsibility of the parents before God to bring the child up in accordance with God's will, that is to say as a person and not as a slave in his parents' service. Now we can see the full meaning of St Paul's words: to possess as if not possessing, that is to say neither abdicating from the authority delegated by God, nor misusing the child as if he were a personal possession.

The Bible, however, is realistic. It has no illusions about the tenacity of the instinct to possess which rules men's hearts. Remember the tragic struggles which Jesus had with the rich and the powerful; remember the severe strictures he addressed to them; remember the well-known story of his encounter with the rich young man, and his reflection on seeing him turn sadly away: 'How hard it is for those who have riches to make their way into the kingdom of God!' And as his disciples were asking, 'In that case who can be saved?' Jesus replied, 'Things that are impossible for men are possible for God' (Luke 18.27).

Obviously this means that in the eyes of Jesus, who knew men's hearts well, man is incapable by himself, by his own moral effort, by his idealism, of liberating himself from his desire to possess. It means that that is possible only in so far as God himself intervenes in his life and liberates him by making him a 'new man' in Christ, as St Paul says. Henri Fesquet writes[8] that our contemporaries no longer feel the need of a saviour because the idea of salvation has lost all meaning for them, since they no longer have any idea of what they ought to be saved from. He suggests calling it liberation instead of salvation. We have here a good example of something from which man cannot be liberated except through Jesus Christ.

In this light, his first Beatitude, 'Happy are the poor in spirit' (i.e., those who are freed from the spirit of possessiveness) – and indeed the whole of the Sermon on the Mount (Matt. 5) – is seen no longer as a moral order which man is meant to establish by his own efforts, sincere though they may be, but rather as a promise by Jesus which is able to transform those who give themselves to him. Then beside the cradle they have prepared for the child they are expecting, and for whom they have chosen a name, I suggest that the parents should pray together,

asking God to deliver them from their natural possessiveness, so that they may be prepared to bring up their child
respecting him as a person. In that humble atmosphere
they will already be able to see in themselves the possessiveness which threatens to ensnare them, amidst their
great joy in having a child.

And so we come back to our subject. I ask a young
woman why she called her baby Francis.

'Oh,' she exclaims, 'we had no choice. That's my
father-in-law's name, and without anyone having to say
so, we knew in advance that if we had a boy he ought to
be called Francis! I understand the way my father-in-law
feels: his grandfather was called Francis, and his grandfather's grandfather. So he always talked about the baby
carrying on the name in his turn.'

Touching, is it not? There is that nice girl, who is no
doubt very acceptable to her father-in-law, but who does
not see that she is acceptable less for herself than for the
function that has devolved upon her of perpetuating the
dynasty. She is quite proud of having done what was
expected of her, and in the enthusiasm of her love she has
no objection to the choice of this name, which she thinks
a very nice one. It does not occur to her that her son
might some day come to dislike his name, reminding him
as it does that he is the heir of a noble line which his
family is so fond of boasting about. He may take more
after his bohemian, easy-going maternal grandfather, but
still have stamped upon him, in his name, the pattern of
his conformist paternal forebears.

Of course I am careful not to raise these questions with

the happy young mother. The time will come for that later, if life itself raises them. And it is very possible that his illustrious name will act as a favourable stimulus in the development of the child as a person. That does not alter the fact that as far as his paternal grandfather is concerned, that child has to bear his name, belongs to him and his family line, as if he had no other. Later on, perhaps, Francis will not be free to choose his own career. Although having a gift for painting, he will have to follow his father and become a doctor. You can see how the dynastic spirit grows out of the possessive spirit, and nourishes it in return.

Though no one may realize it, not even the daughter-in-law, this situation may well have something to do with the difference in social standing of the two families. The other grandparents, being of more modest origin, may well feel it, and be offended, but without daring to say anything. Their daughter is so happy in her marriage, and is so glad to be a member of a very respectable family, that she feels nothing but pride in having her son bear such an honoured name. Only later may she realize that her child belongs more to her in-laws than to herself, that her views about his future carry no weight, that her patriarchal father-in-law, and even her husband, are humiliating her without realizing that they are doing so.

Over-subtle, you think? Say rather that it is very common. A common problem, seen as it is just beginning, still apparently insignificant. For a marriage is not only a private matter between two lovers who have to adapt their own characters to each other, but the coming together of two families, each with its own traditions and its own life-style. This confrontation is unavoidable. For all that, it must be recognized and resolutely faced by husband and wife together, and taken into account on the occasion of every important decision.

It is just this dialogue between them that has been missing, since our young couple did not have to choose a name for their child. It was imposed in advance by a possessive grandfather. Quite possibly they would finally have chosen the same name themselves. Quite possibly the husband would have said to his wife, 'Listen, we just can't hurt Father by having any other name.' At least he would have expressed the thought, perhaps become aware to some extent of his emotional dependence upon his parents, and perhaps admitted that his father's authority had been weighing heavily upon him and he dared not break away from it. Again, perhaps he would have remembered the divine order laid down in the Bible: 'A man leaves his father and mother and joins himself to his wife, and they become one body' (Gen. 2.24).

Those parents have been deprived of their right together to choose the name of their child. Countless marital difficulties arise when one or other of the partners has not broken free, or has not been able to break free, from the possessiveness of their parents before the marriage, or as the result of the marriage. A young couple can become aware of this kind of dependence if there is a real dialogue in their marriage, and even before, during the period of the engagement.

Moreover, such a dependence can be even more unconscious than in the case I have just described. A young couple say naively that they really do not know what name to choose, whereas in reality they are afraid of saying what they think, for fear that the name will not be acceptable to their respective parents.

But of course factors of a more personal nature may inhibit the dialogue. In the joyous exaltation of the honeymoon it seems easy to agree. A young wife exclaims, 'It's fantastic how alike we are! We have the same tastes, the same interests, the same opinions.' Let her enjoy her happiness. It is the miracle of love, at any rate of its first quite normal stage. That young woman is so much in love with her husband that she thinks all he says is wonderful and all his suggestions marvellous. For example, when he suggests a name for the baby she is expecting she unhesitatingly applauds his choice. No other name would have pleased her more.

That husband and wife are still singing in unison. For them the real dialogue has not begun. It will come when they see that they are more different from each other than they thought. One day perhaps that wife will complain to her husband, 'I'm not myself any more. You have moulded me in your image. You have imposed all your likes and dislikes and all your opinions on me. I've had to give up lots of things I liked to do because you didn't like them. I've had enough.' It is like a thunderclap out of a clear sky. The husband is astonished. 'That's not true,' he says, 'we have always agreed so well together! You never told me you didn't agree. Give me some examples.'

And when she tries to think of examples the wife realizes that she has for a long time been harbouring grievances and complaints which she has been careful not to express – not because she was afraid to do so, she thinks, but for the sake of peace and for fear of spoiling the happy harmony that has existed between her and her husband.

What was the good of starting arguments, she said to herself, and disturbing the atmosphere of their home? She had to accept her husband as he was, and be conciliatory; happiness in their marriage was well worth a few sacrifices! And so, gradually, imperceptibly, from the best of motives rather than the worst, she had become withdrawn and separate from her husband, and had lost the very treasure she had wanted to preserve. Her husband did not like her friend Denise, and so she stopped seeing her, or saw her only in secret. He was not fond of music, and so she had given up going to concerts. She would not have enjoyed going without him.

It is not easy to assert oneself without crushing somebody else, to be true to oneself without coming into conflict with others. It is not much easier in the restricted family circle than in politics or the church. So, for instance, this wife for her part was not very fond of one of her husband's friends, who had never accepted her, and had been openly jealous and critical of her. She considered that this friend had too great a hold over her husband and was a bad influence on him. She said as much to him one day, but the husband had answered indignantly, 'You're not going to separate me from my best friend!'

And she had not insisted. Then he had chosen the friend as godfather to their child, who now bore his name.

There was no dialogue, simply because over and over again she had not wanted to go against her husband. It is not only a matter of the proprieties expected towards a patriarchal grandfather. There are all sorts of social conventions. One of the partners may be very conformist, very sensitive to fashion, and prefer a Christian name that is in vogue at the time, whereas the other would rather have something more original, especially if their surname is a common one. But where is one to draw the line between originality and extravagance in choosing a name – as in choosing a dress? Not everyone draws it in the same place.

The husband, for instance, may have come across an old-fashioned Christian name that he takes a fancy to, in a novel. He is quite proud of his discovery; and it goes so well with their surname. But his wife is particularly afraid of ridicule. You must not make yourself conspicuous. She thinks the name pretentious. In school the other children will laugh at her child and quickly find some grotesque distortion of the name. The best names, she thinks, are those that do not attract attention and criticism. But will the child not be better able to feel the value that his parents attach to him as a person if they give him a less ordinary name?

No one escapes this problem, certainly not those best of parents who respect the person of their child, who care about his future, and who want to bring him up for himself, and not for their personal satisfaction. Nevertheless, however generous their care for him, they can judge only in the light of their own personal inclinations. Now, though we saw just now that in the first flush of their love the differences between the partners may be blotted out, in the long run they are almost bound to react against this and to make accusations against each other, without their love being any less.

C. G. Jung has shown that young men and women are instinctively attracted by a complementary partner, and so one that is very different. Thus an extrovert, sociable woman will attach herself to an introverted man, whose depth of mind is a revelation to her. This applies to all departments of life, so that one partner will be more spendthrift and the other more economical, one more open and the other more secretive, one more gay and the other more morose, one stricter and the other more liberal, one more whimsical and the other more method-ical, one more bold and the other more timid, one more sentimental and the other more rational. A day may come when the husband's thrift irritates his extravagant wife. In her eyes it is no longer a virtue, but a vice. She thinks him mean, selfish and miserly. She begins to spend foolishly as a reaction to her husband's miserliness! Each accentuates his or her natural tendency in opposition to the other.

I remember one incident which brought home to me the absurdity of this counterbalance mechanism. My wife was stricter than I in the upbringing of the children. And the stricter she was, the more indulgent I became. Even when I ought to have been severe I refrained. The children were scolded enough without my adding reprimands of my own. Thus my attitude was not merely compensatory, but a way of lecturing my wife. The more passive I was, the stricter she became. She had, as it were, to be severe enough for two.

One morning in the silence of my daily meditation, I realized the absurdity of this reciprocal conditioning, and made a note that I must do better at fulfilling my responsibilities in the upbringing of the children. When I spoke of it to my wife, she was greatly relieved. 'That means,' she said with a happy smile, 'that I can be less strict if you are more so.' Therefore it is not a matter of suppressing the differences between husband and wife, but of stopping the exaggeration of them either as a counterbalance or through obstinacy. What they must do is together to seek freely the best course moment by moment, to be open with each other, and to enter into dialogue. Respect for the person of the child begins with respect for that of the marriage partner.

The search for a name for the child is an excellent occasion for such a dialogue. All our natural inclinations, all our complexes, innate or acquired, manifest themselves in all our judgments. Some choose immediately and intuitively, without quite knowing why, and then find plenty of reasons to support their choice. Others hesitate for a long time, weigh the pros and cons, and as soon as their choice is made start wondering if they ought not to have made a different choice.

Of course this does not apply only to the names we give our children. When we were having our present house built, we were wondering what name to baptize it with. Close by there was a very fine oak tree; but 'Old Oak' or 'Great Oak' seemed terribly hackneyed! One day as I was looking at the wheatfields ripening on the other side of the villa, I got an idea – 'The Grain of Wheat'. I liked it, but remained uncertain and undecided, and put off mentioning it to my wife. How would she react? It was as much her house as mine. And how would it strike my friends? Too heavy a biblical allusion? But I am greatly relieved that it has been so well received. And what of the titles I give to my books? They too are like the names of children. Several have been chosen by my publishers, who are as it were the godparents of these children of mine.

3

Why This Name?

What is it that makes us like one name and dislike another? It is said that there is no accounting for taste. True, but one can enter into dialogue, that is to say one can analyse, try to understand – to understand oneself as well as others. Generally a name reminds us of someone, of people we have known and perhaps liked, or even disliked. Once again we see how closely the name is bound up with the person. To want our child to bear the same name as some person we have greatly admired and loved, is this not to show an unconscious hope that the child will resemble that person?

Ought not parents to talk about this to their children more often, and frankly explain to them the thoughts and feelings that guided them in choosing the name they did? I ask myself this because of an incident that occurred this very day. We were having lunch in a restaurant. My wife, who suffers from having a very silent husband, readily starts conversations with strangers at the next table. I am too shy, and am always surprised how interesting these impromptu conversations turn out to be. Today it was with a pleasant-looking young woman who was eating a fondue – a Swiss speciality. We learned first that she was unmarried, that she accepted her spinsterhood, and was determined not to give the impression of being an embittered 'old maid'. Then that she worked in Geneva, but was still very attached to her mountain canton, to which she returned every weekend.

The conversation eventually turned to the subject of this book that I am writing. The young woman said at once, 'I must tell you one of my childhood memories.' So that the reader may understand the story, I must first explain that Switzerland is a confederation in which twenty-five small republics, the cantons, enjoy considerable autonomy, each having its parliament, its government and its own laws. Consequently there are some cantons, especially the urban ones, which are to the left in politics, while others, the mountain cantons, are conservative. When our new friend was a little girl in her distant village there was a disturbance in Geneva, led by a left-wing leader called Léon Nicole. He had been sent to prison, but shortly afterwards the people had elected him to the government, a singular event which had occasioned severe criticism in conservative cantons such as that of this young woman.

'My name is Nicole,' she told us, 'and on that day my mother called me from the window while I was playing with some little friends. On hearing my name, one of them shouted an insult at me. He was angry that I should have the same name as the Geneva communist whom his parents detested. I went crying into the house and shouted at my mother, "What did you call me Nicole for?" But she told me very quietly that she hadn't chosen the name in honour of the political leader in Geneva. He had not been heard of then. It was in memory of an old friend she had greatly loved and admired. She talked to me for a long time about her happy memories of her friend. I was touched by what she told me, and quite consoled!'

Sometimes parents choose, not the name of an old friend, but that of some famous personage, a cinema star, a sports champion, the hero of an opera or a novel, or of a popular song of the day. In such cases one should bear in mind that a name lasts a whole lifetime, whereas fashions quickly change. Names may also be chosen for their etymological significance. We are told that Margaret comes from the Greek, and means 'pearl', that a certain Japanese first name means 'lotus flower', or that there is an American Indian name that means 'great black eagle'. We have all delved into this exotic folklore when inventing names for people in our childhood games. Or else a name suggests itself by reason of some special circumstance – Noel for a boy born on Christmas Day, or June for a girl born in that month. When Pharaoh's daughter saved a baby she found floating in his cradle in the Nile, she gave him the name Moses, which means 'taken out of the water' (Ex. 2.10).

In addition there are choices dictated by passion. You will recall the terrible maternal rivalry which set against each other Leah and Rachel, the daughters of Laban and wives of the patriarch Jacob (Gen. 30). True, there was some excuse for them. Their father had deceived Jacob in first giving him Leah, the elder, in place of Rachel whom Jacob loved. As it turned out, the beloved Rachel was barren, whereas Leah gave Jacob four sons one after another. Rachel cannot stand it any longer. She has recourse to a stratagem, making her husband lie with her servant Bilhah, and then having Bilhah give birth on her own knees so that she could claim to be the mother of the child thus brought into the world!

In accordance with a psychological phenomenon which belongs to all ages, including our own, she attributes the success of this scandalous proceeding to God's blessing, exclaiming, 'God has done me justice; yes, he has heard my prayer and given me a son.' Now she too possesses a son, and flaunts the fact before her sister. Note again how possessiveness allies itself with slavery. For in doing as she wills with her servant, even to stealing her child, she is treating her as a slave. Rachel is only able to possess a son because she possesses a slave-girl. Her sister Leah is not to be outdone, and she too gives her servant, Zilpah, to the patriarch, so as to have a son by proxy. Later she once again obtains Jacob's favours by means of a doubtful transaction with her sister involving some mandrakes – reputed to have aphrodisiac qualities. Once again the success of the operation is attributed to God, for Leah says, 'God has paid me my wages for giving my slave-girl to my husband.'

Of course these stories, which moreover may be found among other peoples than Israel, are set in a period when barrenness was looked upon as the supreme curse, and in which the Bible described human beings with a realism unsurpassed even by our pessimistic literature of today. But there could be no clearer picture of the monstrous and inextricable tangle of sexual and maternal or paternal love, of possessiveness and jealousy, which enmeshes the human heart.

The names given to Jacob's twelve sons, which were to become the names of the twelve tribes of Israel, form a sort of signature to the whole sombre story. Read again the passage I have just been quoting, in which Rachel proclaims her joy at having a son, appropriating to herself the son of her servant and looking on him as a gift from God. The Bible adds, 'accordingly she named him Dan'. Dan means judgment or justice. It is a name, therefore, which expresses the passions of the mother and her quite unjust pretensions, chosen in order to express them. The same is no doubt true of the names of the rest of Jacob's sons, whether they were born of Leah, of Rachel, or of their two slave-girls.

I took the trouble to check on this from Professor Martin-Achard, one of those charged with the ecumenical translation of the Bible. One may still hesitate and argue, he tells me, over the exact meaning of certain biblical personal names, because their etymology is not always certain, but they derive in some measure from popular allusions or plays on words. It is easy to understand a play on words in one's mother tongue, but more difficult in a foreign language, even when one knows it well.

There is, however, no doubt that a large number of the personal names in the Bible express the passions, emotions, or feelings of the parents who chose them. This is the case, for example, with the prophet Samuel. This too is a story of jealousy between two women, Hannah and Peninnah, the wives of Elkanah. Peninnah has children but Hannah is barren. The latter, instead of having recourse to pretence, asks Yahweh to grant her a son. Her prayer is answered, and she calls her son Samuel, 'since', she says, 'I asked Yahweh for him' (I Sam. 1.20). This is in fact the meaning of the name. And Samuel became a prophet, thus fulfilling his mother's vow. It is often one of the effects of maternal possessiveness that it determines the vocation of the child.

It is also the case, as we have seen, with the sons of Jacob, named by their respective mothers, in a naive and passionate attempt to outbid each other, it would seem, with ever more triumphant names. The only one of Jacob's sons who received his name from his father was the last, Benjamin (Gen. 35.18), since Rachel his mother died in giving birth to him. And so it was Benjamin of whom Jacob was to be fondest. Jacob himself changed his name. His new name, Israel (Gen. 32.29), also has its meaning, since it recalls Jacob's struggle with God. Such was the tragic destiny of Rachel who so longed to possess a child, and who died as a result. Tragic, too, was the destiny of Israel and his people, who have brought us the highest revelations of God, while fighting constantly against him! Perhaps because the supreme personal contact is combat.

You see how closely our emotional life, as well as our destiny, is bound up with this problem of the name that we are studying here. For instance, a sentimental motive also sometimes prompts parents to give a child the name of another child they have previously lost. This is understandable – they liked the name, and are using it again. But they are also trying in some way to bring back, if not the departed child, at least the familiar name to which their memories of him are attached. For that very reason it is no longer a new name; it evokes the person of the departed, and the younger child who is now to bear it will be unable to avoid the feeling that he is being identified or compared with the now dead older brother. His name will be less personal to himself.

This wish to rescue a name from oblivion, to avoid its extinction, is what lies behind the prescription in the law of Moses that if a man dies childless his brother should marry the widow in order to ensure that he has descendants. The behaviour of Onan (Gen. 38.9) in evading this duty is easier to understand in the light of these considerations. What is clear is the tremendous importance of the name – of the forename, or as here of the surname – an importance so great that there is a strong psychological drive to preserve it when the bearer of it has died. It is a sort of refusal to accept death. This is also why the family of someone killed in a battle or a disaster is so keen to recover the body, so that his name may be recorded on a gravestone or funeral urn.

All this confirms the views of modern psychoanalysts who have shown that our choices, though apparently objective, have their source in our emotional and affective life. And often this affective motivation is less conscious than was the case with Rachel and Leah. The dialogue between the marriage partners as they discuss what name to choose for their child may suddenly bring the motivation to light – 'What does that name remind you of?'

Incidents from the past may be remembered, and as they talk about them they see the effect they have had, and still have, on them. The conversation takes on the nature of a session of psychological analysis. Memories rise to the surface, emotions revive with surprising intensity. The couple thought they were discussing coolly on an aesthetic level whether a certain name was beautiful or not, and they discover how deeply they, like the rest of us, are conditioned by their emotional lives.

So when parents are looking for a name for the child they are expecting, the names that come into their minds, both boys' names and girls' names, the names that attract them, and the name they eventually adopt, never come to them as the result of chance. Nevertheless the determinism at work here often remains more unconscious than I have so far described it. It is bound up with irrational associations of ideas that are inconsequential and improbable at first sight. However, since Freud, no one doubts any more the existence of these dark factors which without our knowledge determine our conscious thoughts.

'One cannot make a number occur to one at one's own free choice any more than a name,' wrote Freud.[1] Psychological analysis would always reveal it to be 'strictly determined'. These opinions were thought revolutionary at the time, but now they have triumphed. Even if the various schools of thought have differing ideas of the nature of our unconscious, they all admit that it plays a more important role in our behaviour than do our conscious thoughts. How powerful our inner resistance always is to the recognition of the determinisms at work within us! We are all more ready to spot the unconscious motivations of others than we are to see our own.

For example, Freud quotes the case of one of Adler's patients who had thought at random of the number 1,734, while his wife had for her part thought of the number 117. He comments, 'Though unable to find any determining reason for his own choice of number, this man was able at once to see why his wife had made the supposedly arbitrary choice she had.' This observation must remind us of Jesus' words when he said that we are all more ready to see the splinter in our brother's eye than the plank in our own. This is surely the cause of many marital conflicts, and it is remarkable how one sees in such cases a head-on clash between two interpretations of the same facts, both equally plausible. But here too the conjugal dialogue can help, so long as we are really ready to listen to what our partners say about us, instead of seeking to defend ourselves against their interpretation of the facts.

Their interpretation! Yes, of course, any psychological analysis can only ever be a hypothesis, accredited by the reasonableness of its deductions, as Paul Ricoeur has so clearly shown.[2] And any interpretation depends as much on the psychological mechanisms at work in the interpreter himself as on those of his patient. I imagine that this is why we have different schools of thought opposing each other. A Freudian interpretation comes spontaneously into the mind of a Freudian psychologist, and a Jungian interpretation into the mind of a follower of Jung.

Thus Dr Louis Kling,[3] of Strasbourg, has suggested a Jungian interpretation of a confession that Freud himself made in a letter to Jung written in 1909. He was writing of his conviction that he would die at the age of sixty-one or sixty-two, and of the painful feeling he had had during a visit to Greece, that he was coming across these two numbers everywhere, like an obsession. He was trying to find an explanation, which obviously would be in accordance with Freudian principles, while Dr Kling gives one after his own fashion, based on Jung's theory of the symbolism of numbers. For my part, I incline to the view that as in deciphering a dream, several different interpretations are possible, all equally valuable, and that our unconscious minds can form a synthesis of a number of different drives.

However that may be, since Freud's work on affective transfer, psychoanalysts think that the most important thing is not interpretation, but the bond that is established between doctor and patient. Jung, who had devoted himself so passionately to the elaboration of subtle, ingenious and sometimes enormously detailed interpretations of dreams, wondered towards the end of his life whether one ought not modestly to content oneself with seeing dreams simply as a doorway through which access might be gained to the deep basic problems of the person.

When what we are concerned with is not psychoanalysis but a dialogue between married partners, there is all the more reason why interpretations should be left to psychological science, where they belong, in favour of the more essential exploration and sharing of personal problems. I make this comparison between psychotherapy and conjugal dialogue because both must be carried out in the same spirit if they are to bear fruit. This psychological spirit consists essentially in getting away from making judgments on behaviour and opinions, which only result in barren arguments, and concentrating on the motivation behind them.

So we no longer hear, 'My husband is mean, and I find it most unpleasant,' but instead, 'Why has my husband become mean?' No longer, 'My wife is too strict,' but 'Why is she so strict and I not strict enough?' No longer, 'I can think of nothing but boys' names,' but 'Why can I think only of boys' names? Isn't it because I want this baby to be a boy? And why do I want it to be a boy and not a girl?' No longer, 'I want him to be called Francis,' but 'Why do I prefer that name?'

So, you see, we have come back to the theme of this book. Questions of this sort can be explored in depth through dialogue; husband and wife can learn mutual understanding. The wonderful thing is that the dialogue begins long before the birth of the baby, at the moment when the person of the child enters the thoughts of the parents and they prepare to welcome him.

The dialogue is a preparation for the great event of the birth — the arrival on the scene of the third person, who will revolutionize the relationship between the parents. What is their attitude to each other which will determine the family climate into which the child will be received? What will be the basic attitude of each of them towards the child? Will he be only an object of personal satisfaction, a being with which they can do as they like, or a person to be respected from the very first day, respected as having a right to be himself? Even further, what is the attitude of the parents already, at this moment, before he is born, to this child? The whole fate of the child hangs on the answer to that question.

The truth of this can be demonstrated by a story I have already told in one of my books, but which will bear repeating here, since it well illustrates the point I am making.

Many years ago I was asked to give a talk on the medicine of the person at Grasse, a small village near Nice in the south of France with a reputation for rose-growing. It was the no less spectacular mimosa season.

The conference was organized by two surgeon friends from Marseille, Dr Pierre Granjon and Dr Jacques Dor. Both have been appointed to professorships since then. On this occasion Dr Dor delivered a brilliant opening lecture on 'the surgery of the person', in which he affirmed that surgery is not merely a technical matter, but also and equally a very personal relationship between the specialist and his patient.

In an article Dr Dor[4] has also remarked how important

it is that the doctor should remember the name of each of his patients and that he should use it when talking to the patient instead of using the name of his disease or the number of his hospital bed. It is easy to forget names when one is more interested in the case than in the person, and patients are very sensitive to this. Let me add that it is no less important that patients should know their doctor's name, which is not always the case in hospitals.

We know how painful was the impression received by those who entered concentration camps, in which numbers replaced names. It is not unknown for proud fathers of large families to introduce their offspring, not by name, but by their number in order of birth. Such children may feel that they are only there to make up the numbers.

Dr Dor himself came from the village of Grasse. My wife and I were welcomed into his family home, a large patriarchal dwelling in which four generations lived in joyous harmony. The atmosphere was full of the charm and the security of the solid traditions of 'Old France'.

Charming, too, was the village meeting-hall, where in somewhat cramped conditions I was to speak to an indulgent audience which was certainly not drawn there either by my name or by the subject on which I was to speak, but rather by their love and respect for this surgeon who was in the chair, a local boy whose success in the academic field was an honour to his birth-place.

In introducing me, Dr Dor was at pains to make clear to the audience what the expression 'medicine of the person' means to us. For it conjures up for us the mystery of the person, which gives to medicine, already rich through its science and its technology, a still greater dimension, which no longer depends on intellectual objectivity, but springs from the heart.

In order to bring his point home Dr Dor told the story I am about to relate here, and which we both had from the lips of Dr Paul Plattner, to whom the incident occurred when he was practising as a psychiatrist in Berne. The law in Switzerland authorizes termination of pregnancy in exceptional cases, and each canton designates experts to whom doctors must refer cases for approval, termed a 'concurrent opinion'.

It was for this purpose that a certain woman visited Dr Plattner. She must have felt that he was not disposed to grant her the 'concurrent opinion' she was asking for, and she tried to plead her cause: 'After all, doctor, it's not all that important! It's only a little bundle of cells!' Surely, in talking to a doctor one is at liberty to use in this way the cold realistic language of science, which calls things by their proper names.

I agree that this manner of speaking is vitally important to us when what we are doing is to express and develop our objective knowledge of the world, our intellectual understanding of things. But it can also help us to conceal from ourselves the other aspect of the world – the world of persons. Or else it permits us to forget it, without our realizing it.

Of course the foetus begins as a little group of cells. We may even say that however much it grows it remains a group of cells all its life. That remains true whatever marvels of organization and function science reveals in it.

So Virchow[5] was able triumphantly to assert that he had spent his life dissecting human bodies and had never yet found any trace of a soul on the point of his scalpel. Similarly, Dr Jacques Monod[6] never found the human person and its essential liberty in his molecular biology test-tubes.

Even scientific psychologists are greatly embarrassed by the concept of the person, defying as it does all attempts at precise definition. They can define the ego, the id, the superego, the shadow, and even Jung's 'persona', which is something quite different, namely the social mask behind which the person hides. The person necessarily eludes them, as Charles Baudouin points out.[7] Science depersonalizes man, as two great thinkers, William James[8] and after him Alexis Carrel,[9] have said.

But let us return to Dr Plattner's consultation. He asked that young mother one small question: 'If you were to keep your baby, what name would you give it?' There was a long silence. Then suddenly the woman rose and said, 'Thank you, doctor, I'll keep it.'

Telling us this story, Dr Plattner added, 'During that long silence I was watching that young woman. She was visibly overcome. I had the feeling that I was witnessing the birth of the person of her child.' It was true – a person had in some way come into existence in that mother's mind when she thought of the name she might one day give to the child. It was no longer a 'little bundle of cells'. It was a living person entrusted to her love, with all the fragile mystery of hopes and cares that goes to make up a human life.

Clearly there was a discontinuity, a sudden leap forward in the inner vision that that mother had, beyond the frontiers of objective scientific knowledge. Her child was no longer a thing, but a personal being who would one day answer to his own name. The name called forth her love by giving it an object.

You can understand why Professor Viktor Frankl[10] insisted on these frontiers of science where the study of man is concerned. Science, he said, is true in all it observes and describes in regard to man and his behaviour, but it lies when it insinuates that man is just that and nothing more. It is right, for instance, when it says that man is a robot, comparable with a computer, but wrong if it claims that man is nothing but a robot. He is 'something more'.

Many doctors feel this to be true, and try to find out what that 'something more' is, which no particular science can show him. A need has been felt for synthesis after so much analysis, and the most hopeful sign of it is the advent of psychosomatic medicine. But whether medicine is organic or psychosomatic, the 'something more' which is the person still eludes it, because the person is of a different order altogether. The person is not the sum of all our knowledge about man. It transcends it at a stroke, as we saw in the instance recounted by Dr Plattner.

If we hope to discover the meaning of the person by adding together all our sciences – anatomy, physiology, psychology, molecular biology, sociology and all the clinical specialities – we shall only end up with a gigantic and still incomplete compendium. It would be extremely complicated, whereas everyone feels that the person is extremely simple, something that can be grasped at once.

The person is an indivisible whole, as Professor Pouyanne of Bordeaux writes.[11] It is not the result of a laborious and unending synthesis, but is given straight off with all its still veiled richness, of which one goes on discovering endlessly more and more.

So how shall we define it? Is there a single word that will adequately express it? Our story teaches us that there is – the name, which is not only the symbol of the person: it is the person itself. What, then, are the characteristics of the person? They are its liberty, its capacity for responsible commitment. And what must we do to contract such a commitment, whether it be a contract of employment, an insurance policy, a will, publishing a book or exhibiting a picture? We must sign it with our name.

So the name signifies the person. Everyone knows, for example, the prayer 'Our father' (Matt. 6.9): 'Hallowed be your name.' An ecumenical French translation of the Bible has just appeared, the result of collaboration between Catholic and Protestant theologians – a remarkable event. No doubt the translators felt that the traditional formula was scarcely likely to be understood any more by our contemporaries. So they have boldly translated it afresh as 'Make yourself recognized as God.'

Of course that is what the prayer means, but our ears tend to be shocked when a change is made in an expression so consecrated by tradition. And one can also try, as I am doing here, to make clear that the name in question now is the person of God himself, whose holiness must be honoured.

Many biblical passages can be seen in a new light once we understand that the name is the person. So when the apostles Peter and John (Acts 4.10–12) appeared before the Sanhedrin and were asked by what power or what name they had healed a crippled man, St Peter replied, 'It was by the name of Jesus Christ the Nazarene.' He goes on, 'Of all the names in the world given to men, this is the only one by which we can be saved.' Now, God's gift for the salvation of men is the person of Jesus Christ. Or again, when St Paul writes to the Philippians that God has raised up Jesus because of his obedience even to death on the cross, and that he has given him 'the name which is above all other names', he is asserting the primacy of his person over all other persons. Remember also Jesus' words: 'Where two or three meet in my name, I shall be there with them' (Matt. 18.20).

There is, however, another passage which I cannot omit to quote here. When the apostles came back to Jesus, full of enthusiasm after their mission, he shared their joy. But he said: 'Yet do not rejoice that the spirits submit to you; rejoice that your names are written in heaven' (Luke 10.20). St Paul echoes him when, writing to the Philippians about his fellow-workers he says, 'Their names are written in the book of life' (Phil. 4.3).

In the Revelation St John, too, speaks of this book of life in which the victor's name is inscribed: 'I shall not blot their names out' (Rev. 3.5). And elsewhere he speaks of 'those who are listed in the Lamb's book of life' (Rev. 21.27).

The name is indeed the person. The resurrection which the gospel proclaims is a personal resurrection – the resurrection of the person. The body will be changed: it will rise 'imperishable' (I Cor. 15.42). The disciples did not recognize the risen body of Christ; and Mary Magdalene did not recognize him until he called her by her name (John 20.16). The psychic make-up will be changed, liberated from all the infirmities which affect it in this world. What remains, or rather what is raised beyond the death which destroys the psychosomatic organism, is the person, the name inscribed in heaven, which will not be blotted out.

Shall we be able to recognize each other? The Rev. Fr Maurice Zundel[12] asks the question in fact in relation to the child 'still hidden in the womb', whose features are still unknown to us, and yet he already has a name. But many people ask it in relation to the resurrection. Yes, we shall recognize each other as persons, by the name which is not blotted out. I am reminded of a piece of testimony which touched me deeply. I was being visited by a colleague who had come from a distant country, and he said to me, 'Before I left one of my friends remarked to me, "You're going to Switzerland, and you will have a chance to see Paul Tournier. No doubt I shall never see him in this world, but tell him from me that he will be one of the first people I shall look out for in heaven." '

The name is the person, and that is what made Dr Plaṭtner say that he had felt he was witnessing the birth of a person. When that mother gave a name in her mind to her child, she made him a person in her own eyes, a person whose life no longer belonged to her, whose life must be respected. We may say that man experiences two births, a biological birth as an organism, and a spiritual birth as a person. For man belongs at the same time to two worlds – the anonymous, impersonal, irresponsible world of nature, and the world of the person, of the spirit, filled with meanings and responsibilities.

In the famous passage in which Martin Buber[13] contrasts the 'I – thou' relationship with the objective 'I – it' relationship, he takes as an example not, as one might have expected, a human being, but a tree. In saying 'thou' to the tree, he turns it from being a thing, an object of scientific observation or of aesthetic admiration, into a subject, a person, a partner in a personal relationship. It is as if he were giving it a proper name.

In speaking therefore of two distinct worlds, the world of persons and the world of things, I am not meaning to set the human race over against the rest of creation. I mean two modes of seeing and feeling the whole world. It is possible to treat people as things, and a tree as a person – addressing it as 'thou' as Martin Buber did.

When man received from God the power to give names, he thus received a double power. On the one hand by giving proper names he creates persons, he peoples the world with persons, he personalizes the world, making it a great symphony of responsible persons; on the other hand, by giving scientific common names, he turns the world into an anonymous round of irresponsible things, and even turns man into a thing as all the 'human sciences' do. Bertrand de Jouvenel,[14] quoting Laberthonnière, attributes to Descartes the genesis of the attitude which turns the whole of nature into things, 'an attitude which favours the material possession of the world'.

There is no need to choose between these approaches nor to oppose the one to the other. We should see in them man's double vocation. He can look upon the world as a great blind machine, and upon himself as a machine, and upon his psychology as the impersonal interplay of rigorously determined phenomena. We know how fruitful this view has been in the development of science and of the intellectual understanding of the world.

But he can also look upon himself, upon his child and upon all other human beings, all the heavenly bodies and every single thing as persons with whom he establishes a personal and responsible relationship. So when Francis of Assisi in his wonderful poetry spoke to 'brother sun' and 'brother wolf', he turned them into persons, partners in spiritual fellowship. 'Faith always implies relationship with a person,' writes Denis V. Martin.[15]

An engine-driver calls his locomotive Beatrice. From then on it is no more just a locomotive for him, but a familiar friend who has her whims and her thirst to be loved and pampered. He talks to her as he oils her joints, and when he polishes her it is like a caress. A woman whose life has been tragically restricted by sickness suddenly tells me of her decision to learn to drive and buy a car. I see in this the success of my colleagues who have been treating her: she is beginning to emerge from her long period of trial. Then I ask her, 'What name will you give to your car?' – 'I shall call it Hope.' She has bought the car and given it its name. She sends us a piece of the christening-cake in a box inscribed with the name: Hope. We savour it joyfully, for it is a sign that that woman has been born into a more personal life herself. From now on she will travel with hope. She has visited us with Hope – we were both greatly moved!

We may well see in these two approaches, the intellectual approach of common names and the affective approach of proper names, the mark of the two principles, the masculine and the feminine, which together form human nature, and which Jung called *animus* and *anima*. The first, the *logos*, calls things by their scientific names in order to define them properly and to identify the relationships of cause and effect which bind them together. The second, the *eros*, or love, addresses them as 'thou' and gives them proper names to make them into persons and establish personal links with them.

Moreover, women in general have the sense of the person much more than men have. This means that they have a special mission, which is to reintroduce love, to give back its humanity to a world which remains so glacial when men alone have built it. However that may be, the two approaches, the logical and the spiritual, are equally legitimate and necessary. Only, the relative preponderance of one or the other varies from age to age. Our present civilization is too masculine, dominated as it is by reason, science and technology, to such an extent that everything seems to consist of biological or social phenomena, almighty but meaningless. Man feels himself to be a robot and no longer a person. All he sees is the determinism of his instincts and drives, and that of economic forces.

Then all at once, in this boring and rigid society, an unexpected light can break forth from a personal encounter; in particular from the encounter with God, who is, as Viktor Frankl says,[16] the person *par excellence*, or, in Martin Buber's words,[17] 'the only Thou who by his very nature can never become an It'. Then the world is seen in a different light. Man becomes aware once more that he is a person, and discovers the world of persons all around him. His own life takes on meaning again, and the world itself takes on meaning in his eyes. He recovers his aptitude and feeling for personal contact. This happened to me at the age of thirty-four.

It may be that a man who has hitherto been entirely absorbed in an exacting and monotonous career suddenly falls in love. He too feels himself transformed by love, and becomes once more a person willing to give himself.

But with marriage he will have to return quickly to more down-to-earth preoccupations – finding a house, working out a budget, getting down to the indispensable daily routine. Then all at once his wife is pregnant. The child she is carrying is once again a person breaking into his life and transfiguring it.

That child is not just the outcome of a biological process, a little bundle of cells. He is a person. Spontaneously a name is sought for him. It is necessary to be able to call him by his name, well before he is capable of answering to it. That name already contains a future that is mysterious in that it will without any doubt turn out quite differently from anything the parents can imagine. But in calling him by his name they are already entering into dialogue with him, recognizing him as a person. And that little child is already responding to them: he is calling them to become aware once more of themselves as responsible persons.

In this way, even before the child's birth, his personal relationship with his parents is in preparation. It will contribute more than anything else to his development. The world of persons has in fact priority over the world of things for the very small child. Striking evidence of this is provided by an observation made by Dr René Spitz.[18] He notes that a baby recognizes his mother's face two months before recognizing his feeding-bottle, despite its being a very familiar and gratifying 'thing'.

This same specialist goes on to point out the decisive importance for the infant's future of the 'affective climate' of his relationship with his mother. The expression is a good one, but it is important to see that it is not only the visible manifestations of affection which determine the climate, but also the basic inner attitude of the mother towards her child, who is very quick to sense it. In other words, what matters is the quality of the mother's love.

If the mother's love has no other source than the joy of 'having' a child of her own, an 'object' of love, a little 'thing' that is entirely dependent upon her, whose function is to satisfy her maternal instinct, she is introducing into her relationship with the child a suggestion of possessiveness against which he will increasingly have to defend himself, with consequent damage to the 'affective climate'. If, on the other hand, she has been conscious right from the start that the baby is a person, that is to say a unique human being who must become himself, the purpose of whose existence is in himself and not in the satisfaction of his parents, then he will feel that he is accepted as a person and will be able himself to accept the love that is offered to him. The important thing in parents who are expecting a child is their capacity to accept the 'other'.

So we have come back to the central theme of this book. But now I must go into it more deeply, and make quite clear all that is involved in respect for the person of the child.

4

The Mother's Voice

My colleague Dr Jean Sarkissoff, of Geneva, has talked to me about his experiments,[1] and they will guide our thoughts. For two years he has been using the method discovered twenty years ago by Professor Tomatis, of Paris. The latter applied it in the treatment of cases of mutism, psychogenic autism and infantile schizophrenia. The doctor plays over to these children a tape-recording of their mother's voice, in which a certain range of sound wave-lengths has been electronically filtered out. The aim of this procedure is to let the child hear his mother's voice more or less as he must have heard it while in her womb.

Next, the filtering is progressively reduced, to the point where he is hearing the mother's voice exactly as he has heard it since birth. Results obtained using this technique have been remarkable. A child who until then has been incapable of communicating at all, abandons his mutism. So that the doctor has succeeded in mobilizing his desire to communicate, by making him hear his mother's voice as he heard it before his birth.

These experiments call our attention to an obvious

fact, namely that the foetus, at least in the later months of intra-uterine life, can hear his mother's voice. Furthermore, it is registered on the engrams of his brain, since he can recognize it, just as Dr Lorenz's baby birds are able to pick out their mother's voice from among all other voices.[2] Yes, you expectant mothers, your unborn baby can hear your voice. He can also hear the beating of your heart and the rhythm of your breathing. He is registering it all for ever in his still unconscious mind – and so firmly is it imprinted there that it is possible by means of an ingenious technique to awaken the memory of it. What does that imply? Does it not confirm what we have already said, that that child is a person long before he is born?

Now, Dr Jean Sarkissoff applies this method to the treatment of neuroses in which psychoanalysis after initial success has proved powerless. The thing that struck me in Dr Sarkissoff's reports was the intense emotion that can be aroused by this hearing of the filtered voice of the mother. Every psychotherapist knows that emotional discharge is the sign of the success of the cure.

However, it is not always possible in the case of adult neurotics to procure a recording of the mother's voice. Dr Sarkissoff turns instead to playing tapes of soft music to the patient, filtered of course in accordance with Professor Tomatis' technique. Here too he obtains a therapeutic effect, albeit less powerful. It is possible, therefore, to argue at length about how much the success of the method owes specifically to recognition of the mother's voice, or whether it is a vague reminiscence of the general audition of filtered sounds as the foetus would hear them, or whether, indeed, it is the effect of the sort of subdued music which is so commonly used today as background music.

The field is open for experiment, and as always in medicine questions of doctrine must be left for the future to throw light upon. The essential thing in medicine is to heal, and frequently procedures have been used before their mechanism is understood, as for example the treatment of anaemia by the ingestion of liver.

I was struck by another aspect of the problems raised by Dr Sarkissoff's researches. This was that the sound of the filtered voice used by Professor Tomatis was a sort of unvoiced rustling, which seemed to me to bear a remarkable resemblance to what is called glossolalia – the 'speaking with tongues' of the New Testament – which played an important part in the primitive Christian church, and which is once again playing an important role in the so-called Pentecostal churches. It is not a real language, because it does not express any intelligible idea. In particular it is not a language that one could invent, learn, or imitate; it bursts forth spontaneously in a certain state of ecstasy.

When I heard it, I understood that it was, so to speak, the expression of the inexpressible. The feelings of the first Christians, on the Day of Pentecost, and later in their assemblies, and the feelings of modern Christians under the influence of the Holy Spirit, are impossible to put into words, and yet they imperiously demand expression.

You remember what St Paul says about glossolalia; he

recognizes it as a gift of the Holy Spirit (I Cor. 12.10), granted to one and not to another, and not to be boasted of as superior to other gifts. He does not hide his preference for intelligible witness: 'Now suppose, my dear brothers, I am someone with the gift of tongues, and I come to visit you, what use shall I be if all my talking reveals nothing new, tells you nothing, and neither inspires nor instructs you?' (I Cor. 14.6).

Nevertheless, St Paul knows that the most convincing revelations cannot be formulated in intellectual discourses or in didactic texts. Such was the revelation which overtook him on the Damascus road. After all his polemics in the second letter to the Corinthians, it is to that ineffable experience that he points in order to establish his spiritual authority (II Cor. 12.2–4). And he points out that he felt it, not as an intellectual and intelligible instruction, but as an almost physical experience: 'whether still in the body or out of the body, I do not know; God knows —' he writes. There could be no clearer indication that what happened was not on the level of lucid thought, but on the mysterious level of the incarnate person. Is it not of that same level that we are speaking – profound, obscure and organic – when we refer to the recording of the mother's voice on the mind of the child she is carrying in her womb?

So it seems that glossolalia under the influence of the Holy Spirit might be a kind of reminiscence of the non-verbal language perceived by the unborn child, which characterizes his total communion with his mother during that happy period. It is one way of being like little

children, as Jesus asks us to be, so as to enter the Kingdom of God (Mark 10.15). And so we return to Dr
Sarkissoff's experiments.

Of course, in his mother's womb the child does not
understand what his mother is saying, but he hears her
voice, and the voice is communication between persons,
independently of the transference of ideas which will
come when the words are understood. The voice is an
even more important and direct non-intellectual instru-
ment of communication than language. For a long time
after his birth, before learning the meanings of words and
phrases, the child will remain extremely sensitive to his
mother's voice. As René Spitz remarks, 'It is scarcely
necessary to add that it is his mother's voice which provides the child with vital acoustic stimuli which form the
basis of the development of speech.' [3]

But beforehand, what counts most for the child, what
he is most sensitive to, is the tone of the maternal voice,
revealing as it does her state of mind. The tone is a kind
of non-verbal language within speech. It goes along with
all the other forms of non-verbal language – the
caresses, kisses, glances, welcoming gestures, the importance of which was stressed by the paediatrician Dr
Jean-Jacques Bindschedler, of Strasbourg, at one of our
conferences on the medicine of the person.

An indissoluble bond is therefore established between
mother and child before the birth, in that happy period
during which nothing separates him from his mother,
when he is aware only of soft and muffled sounds, when
he is wrapped in warmth, and without doing anything

himself he receives food and oxygen, where he can perform tricks like a cosmonaut in a state of weightlessness. It is hardly surprising that so many people, like me, are lazy all their lives, after such an easy start.

With birth, all is changed. Our first contact with the world outside is brutal. The cold, the light, the noise and commotion, the lack of oxygen, the hands of the midwife manipulating the child, sometimes the forceps, the fall into a void, the separation from the mother – everything conspires to make this first turning-point in our lives traumatic. It is noteworthy that one of the earliest psychoanalysts, Rank,[4] suspected that behind all our anxieties, and making us sensitive to them, lies this primitive anxiety experienced at birth.

Many experiments and researches done since then have confirmed this view, and quite recently the Japanese psychiatrist Dr Susumu Akahoshi has formulated a doctrine which obviously derives from it: for him the destiny of the human person is dominated by his first and painful experience, which Akahoshi calls 'basic mistrust'.[5] The phrase signifies a fundamental disappointment of primitive confidence. If I may be permitted a very free and metaphorical translation, I shall call it a disappointment in love. To be disappointed in love is to suffer one of the most serious psychological traumas. It is the most frequent cause of the telephone calls for help to such organizations as the Samaritans.

One can say that human life begins with a terrible disappointment in love. The young man in love who has been 'dropped' by his girlfriend exclaims, 'I can't understand how it could happen – we loved each other so much!' The new-born babe might think the same. Perfect love existed between him and his mother while he was in her womb. And with that perfect love a feeling of security and total confidence in life and love. Then at birth the infant is 'dropped' by his mother.

It is true that Dr Akahoshi does not allude explicitly to the trauma of birth. Quoting E. Erikson's book *Childhood and Society*,[6] he situates the 'basic mistrust', the first experience of confidence deceived, in the first year of life, when the mother disappoints the child's need of total dependence. In fact that total dependence existed during the period of pregnancy, and it is in contrast with that that the child is disappointed. However much the mother loves and cares for her child, she can no longer give him the satisfaction which he experienced in her womb. It is a real disappointment in love.

You know too what the forsaken lover says: 'I won't be caught again! I shall never again be able to believe in love, or trust anyone's assurances of love.' He has at one and the same time an overwhelming need of love and a rooted distrust of it. It is in fact these two reactions which Dr Akahoshi sees as characteristic of our human condition: an intense need of love, or *amae*-reaction (in Japanese *amae* means the need to be loved), and a turning in upon the self, a refusal of the love of others, or *jiritsu* reaction, which corresponds to what Freud called 'narcissism'.

Of course it is in vain that the abandoned lover says that he will never be caught again, that he has lost confidence in love, for you know that despite everything he is longing to rediscover the perfect love he once enjoyed. All human beings are like that, in perpetual quest of perfect love, in quest of 'reparation', to use Melanie Klein's word:[7] reparation of love, of understanding, security and confidence.

The perfect love that existed between mother and child during pregnancy was much more than a feeling, much more than an affective phenomenon. It was a communion of persons. So the 'reparation' which man ceaselessly seeks is not love-feeling, *eros*, but love-communion, *agape*, spiritual love, as Dr Akahoshi tells us.

That also is what the medicine of the person is – helping men and women by the spiritual quality of the love we give them, to experience the love of God. The Japanese psychiatrist goes on to quote the passage in St John's first epistle: 'This is the love I mean: not our love for God, but God's love for us when he sent his son to be the sacrifice that takes our sins away' (I John 4.10). He paraphrases this text in reference to the perfect primitive love between mother and child: 'It was not I who first loved my mother, but she who loved me.'

What does this mean, if not that mankind has at bottom always felt itself to be in search of perfect love, that 'love-communion', and that the sickness *par excellence* of the person is mankind's inner dichotomy between the thirst for love and the refusal of love through resentment at being disappointed in love – a process which starts at birth, which is not only an affective trauma but also a breaking of communion.

Repairing the harm done by a trauma is the easier and the more effective the less violent the trauma has been. Now we can see the full significance of our thoughts on the person of the child and on the respect due to him. Respecting the person of the child means being aware of his sensitiveness, and trying to make his arrival in the world as little traumatic as possible. Such is the aim of Dr Leboyer,[8] a Parisian doctor, in his method which he calls 'natural birth', or more accurately 'birth without violence', and which he has been using for the last five years in his clinic. It is complementary to the 'painless childbirth' which, like it, is true medicine of the person.

Essentially the method consists in not cutting the umbilical cord before its pulse has ceased, so as to avoid any feeling of asphyxiation in the child. In addition to this the strictest precautions are taken to reduce stress: silence, calm, subdued lighting, immediate and prolonged contact by the baby with the mother, so that he can 'get to know her' again. The results are remarkable, according to Dr Leboyer. His new-born infants do not cry, develop better than others, and even smile at the age of two or three days. Perhaps we may hope that later on they will contribute to a reduction in the increasing flood of neurotics pouring in upon doctors and psychotherapists.

I confess that at the time when I was attending confinements I was a little scornful of the sentimentality of the mothers, and I was at pains to show them that their babies were not as fragile as they thought, by handling them with a certain roughness. But those mothers were right to make a fuss of their little ones, and to treat them with extreme gentleness, as if the least touch might break them in two. Mothers are guided by instinct, and doctors who are trying to follow the laws of nature have a lot to learn from them.

Their instinct also teaches them the importance of kisses and of skin-to-skin contact. Remember too that mothers once used to carry their infants for long periods in their arms, at the same time as they attended to the household chores. Their instinct is also tenderly to sing sweet songs to them, and to rock them for hours on end, answering in this way to a need which will give them a lasting love of merry-go-rounds, swings and slides.

Dr René Spitz,[9] the great specialist in infant psychology, puts it in a nutshell: 'We have given up the old rocking cradle, for no valid reason that I can see.' He even suggests the reinstatement of the baby's dummy, once condemned on hygienic grounds, which the investigations of Levine and Bell[10] have shown to be the best treatment for 'three-months colic'.

So the personal relationship of mother and child is of primary importance, a fact neglected by a medicine that has become too technical. Some modern maternity wards have become factories, where everyone is in a hurry, and where babies cry alone in their aseptic boxes parked in rows like cars, from which they are taken only to be put to the breast: an early initiation to the mechanization of modern life. In these days when it is fashionable to be concerned about the environment, we might well take a look at the environment of the newly born.

One of the greatest catastrophes occasioned by modern

social developments is the separation of mother and child when the former returns to paid work. Maternity leave is very short. Mothers ought to be prohibited from going out to work for at least two years after their confinement, so that they can devote their time to their children. At the same time society ought to see that a mother gets the same income she would get if she were working. When we know that the present increasing flood of neuroses is due principally to this deprivation of the maternal presence, it is difficult to understand this gap in social legislation, especially in my own country, where any group of citizens has the 'right of initiative', that is to say the right to propose for popular vote a new clause in the constitution, provided it is supported by a petition containing 50,000 signatures.

However that may be, birth is the major event in all our lives, and it inevitably leaves traces behind, since nothing is lost in the life of the mind. I have already referred to Rank's views on the emotional importance of this event, which he looks upon as possibly the prime source of human anxiety. It is known that Freud rejected Rank's opinion, as have the majority of his school. The most competent of Freud's followers in matters concerning the mind of the infant, namely the American psychoanalyst René Spitz,[11] maintains that the new-born infant is incapable of feeling much at all, 'because he has no Ego . . . he cannot handle the stimuli he receives, and is almost automatically protected from them by his high perceptive threshold'. But Spitz goes on, 'Nevertheless, when the stimuli are sufficiently powerful, they cause a breach in the protective barrier, and this may modify the as yet undifferentiated personality of the infant.'

Where, then, is the threshold for these 'sufficiently powerful' stimuli? It is a matter of conjecture. What do we know of other people's pain? When I was a doctor at the Policlinique Médicale in Geneva, half a century ago, there were many Italians among the destitute patients we had to treat, and they showed great sensitivity to pain. We often argued about it: were these Italians more seriously ill than our Swiss patients, or did they only react more keenly to the same level of pain? It is obvious that we can never measure the pain experienced by any of our patients, but only their reaction to it. How much more true, then, it is in the case of a new-born child who can scarcely express himself at all.

Here Dr René Spitz himself sounds a note of caution: 'The experimental method,' he writes, 'cannot be fully relied upon in this case, and I am compelled to adopt a reconstructive approach.' Which means that what the new-born child really feels, and what he may be aware of, we just do not know. Furthermore, one must not confuse perception with recording in the memory, as Spitz remarks: 'The new-born child does not perceive. Perception properly so-called presupposes self-consciousness, which is not to say that the memory does not retain traces of the thing experienced.'

In fact other psychoanalysts have uncovered memory traces which appear to confirm Rank's theories. 'It is not exceptional,' writes Dr Sarkissoff,[12] 'for patients to go right back in the course of psychoanalysis to memories of their birth, usually after several years of treatment.' The extraordinary thing is that, as Dr Sarkissoff goes on to say, 'with the Tomatis method of listening to the filtered voice of the mother, cases are equally frequent right at the start of the treatment, of conscious recall of the events of birth'.

So it seems that the method acts as a sort of detonator for the explosion of a huge charge of repressed emotion. The author concludes: 'The Tomatis method has convinced me that birth is consciously experienced by the infant.' That is in fact the subject of this book – the mystery of the person which already exists before birth and during birth, even though most of us have lost the memory of it for ever.

You will understand why I pause here to look more closely at these experiments and their significance for our subject. One may ask, in particular, whether it is not just because Dr Sarkissoff is passionately interested in the recall of the emotional shock of birth, that his patients offer him what he seeks. We know in fact that a patient being treated by a Freudian will have more and more 'Freudian' dreams; a follower of Jung will find his patients having 'Jungian' dreams; and a follower of Adler will be offered by his patients more and more 'Adlerian' dreams.

The phenomenon goes much farther. The psychoanalyst Dr Balint[13] has maintained that the patients of ordinary doctors come to them with the sort of organic diseases the doctors are most interested in – apparently without suspecting that in his own case too his patients bring him the diseases he is interested in as a psychoanalyst. One has even got round to wondering whether psychotherapy does not sustain the neurosis at the same time as it treats it. My own patients also bring to me the personal problems and the religious experiences in which I am so keenly interested.

After all, you talk about different things with everyone you meet. When you are telling someone about an experience in your own life, you draw without even realizing it upon memories that will interest him — school memories with a teacher, memories of your relationship with your parents with a psychoanalyst, religious memories with a clergyman or an atheist, memories of law with a lawyer, of philosophy with a philosopher, of stamps with a philatelist, of food with a gourmet, and of market prices with a housewife.

But that does not mean that your memories are not authentic, that your accounts are not faithful ones, that your opinions are not sincerely held, that you have not really had the dream you are recounting. All you are doing is to choose from the infinite reservoir of your mind the things that will interest the person you are speaking to. We can express only what is in us, even to our most extraordinary fantasies, and even to our lies, which are also a kind of truth about us, and when Dr Sarkissoff's patient tells him with overwhelming emotion about the anxiety he experienced at birth, it is just because he has experienced it.

However prodigious the imagination of men, it remains attached to the elements of reality. It can create fictitious worlds only by manipulating in some different way the bits and pieces of the real world. In order to invent fantastic creatures men are reduced to putting wings on a bull or a fish's tail on a woman. Their fantasy universe is like a constructional toy which can be taken to pieces and assembled differently, but still consists of the pieces one has been given to start with; or like a gigantic card game with vast numbers of cards that have all, however, been distributed before the start of the game. They can grasp only what they are able to grasp of the external world, that is to say what they already carry within themselves. They cannot conceive of suffering, joy, anxiety or love, if they have never themselves experienced them. Even God himself is pictured in the Bible as an old man with a beard, whose finger writes his law on tablets of stone (Ex. 31.18).

But the materials in the great constructional game of the mind are also numberless. Our mind is an infinite reservoir the inventory of which it would be impossible for us to make. Stored in it is an unlimited multitude of memories, of which we use only a few scraps with our associations of ideas. I should need the time of a thousand lives to tell the story of the single life I have lived. The human mind is an inexhaustible sack that contains everything – all Jung's archetypes, all Freud's drives, all Adler's overcompensations, all Pavlov's conditioned reflexes, all the vices and all the virtues, the most tenacious hopes and the most complete despairs, the symbols of all religions, all courage and all cowardice, the lucidity of reason and the blindness of passion, and at every moment both life and death.

And so one can find there everything one wants, the confirmation of every psychological doctrine, without on that account proving that the others are false. And so one can understand man in a thousand different ways and from a thousand points of view, without ever completely understanding him. That is the person, the mystery of the person, an unbelievable diversity, and yet a rigorous unity, an absolute singularity, and yet a common nature.

And the child you are expecting, happy parents, to whom you are going to give a name, is already that – a person with his or her innumerable possibilities, of which he will realize just one, his personal life. You will be told that he will form his Ego only later on, in about a year's time, when he learns to distinguish between himself and the external world. Or, as Melanie Klein says,[14] when he is able to see his mother as an 'entire person', and no longer fragmented into a number of 'objects' of satisfaction.

But his person is already there, from before his birth. The Dutch paediatrician Jan van der Hoeven[15] makes a clear distinction between the Ego and the Person. Well before birth the baby has an intuition (*Ahnung*) that he is a person. Thus the person is at one and the same time a primitive and entire datum, and also a perpetual becoming, perpetually uncompleted. The child is a person from before his birth, clothed already in his dignity as a person. And because he is a person he is called to become always more really a person throughout his life. As the old Greek poet Pindar said, 'Become what you are.'

Yes, dear Madam, the child you are expecting is a

person now, in physical, psychic and spiritual evolution. He is already enriching his person with all the sensations he is registering – your warmth, the oxygen you are giving him, the sound of your voice, the rhythm of your heart and your breathing. The drama of birth that we have described and which awaits him, will also be a great human experience without which he cannot become the person he is. You long to save him from all suffering. Using Dr Leboyer's method it will be possible for you to attenuate the anxiety of birth, though not to suppress it altogether.

'To be born is to lose one's mother,' writes Dr Sarkissoff. A line of communication has been broken and from now on the problem is how to re-establish it. The whole future of the person is to be taken up with this problem of establishing communication between persons. Birth is the first frustration and the prototype of all frustrations, all the bereavements which mark out life's course, to use Freud's term. The person will be formed from bereavement to bereavement, from one suffering accepted to another.

That is what the life of the person, spiritual life, is. Dr Sarkissoff speaks of it in another of his books, *Psychanalyse et Spiritualité*.[16] He describes the two possible reactions to frustration. He uses different terms from those of Dr Akahoshi, but the analogy is striking: the *jiritsu*-reaction, narcissism, is the natural reaction of the Ego, of the 'illusion of the Ego', which draws away, believes itself to be separate, looking upon itself as the centre of the universe. The other reaction – reparation,

109

the spiritual life – is the re-establishment of communion, an awareness of being part of the whole, communication restored.

Communication with God, broken by the Fall, and restored by Jesus Christ. The relationship between parents and children, broken by possessiveness and re-established by a miracle of the Holy Spirit. Communion with other human beings, disturbed in neurosis, the exemplary restoration of which between doctor and patient constitutes the essence of psychotherapy.

In the book which was offered to me to mark my seventy-fifth birthday, Dr Paul Plattner[17] wrote on this subject, recalling our now departed mutual friend, Dr Alphonse Maeder of Zurich, who, following his teacher Freud, and his friend Jung, continually sought to understand what happens in 'transfer', that is to say, in the mutual relationship between doctor and patient. Dr Plattner tells us how he passed progressively from Freud's purely affective interpretation, through Jung's theory of dialogue, to a personalist interpretation. He described the person of the psychotherapist successively as a 'psychotherapeutic agent', then as a 'partner', and finally as one 'called'. In Maeder's thought, he says, both doctor and patient are called by a third person who is God.

What happens then is not only the revivifying of the relationship with the parents, not only the discovery of the self through the agency of the doctor, but the experience of communion between persons, between two persons, and between them and the person of God.

In the same book Professor Arthur Jores[18] of Hamburg

also describes the relationship between doctor and patient in the medicine of the whole person. He quotes a Mexican doctor, Dr Seguin, who speaks of a 'psychotherapeutic Eros', saying that this really means the relationship of love which Christ taught, and of which he was the example.

As you see, it all converges, and we come back to the thought of Dr Akahoshi and of Dr Sarkissoff. But of course this 'call' goes beyond the doctor's consulting-room. We have long realized that it is not only neurotics who need to experience communion. Indeed, we know that the whole of our modern world is sick for lack of love, that it has become seriously depersonalized, that men and women feel themselves to be tragically alone in the world. They are treated as units of production, alienated and turned into things, deprived of that personal contact through which we become persons.

What matters, then, is our attitude to others, whether we are possessive towards them, or respect them as persons. That is the question that parents must face from the very first moment when a laboratory report confirms that they are expecting a child – the child to whom they will give a name.

Notes

Chapter 1

1. Aloys von Orelli, *Persönlichkeit, Selbst, Person,* Georg Thieme, Stuttgart 1951.

2. Martin Buber, *I and Thou,* Charles Scribner's Sons, New York 1937.

3. Virgil Gheorghiu, *Pourquoi m' a-t-on appelé Virgil?* Plon, Paris.

4. Georges Gusdorf, *La Parole,* P.U.F., Paris 1953.

5. Konrad Lorenz, *On Aggression,* Harcourt Brace Jovanovich, New York 1966.

6. Marcel Pagnol, *Topaze,* 'Petite Illustration', Barron's Educational Series, Woodbury, N. Y. 1958.

7. Georges Gusdorf, *La découverte de soi,* P.U.F., Paris 1948.

8. Simone de Beauvoir, *The Coming of Age,* G. P. Putnam's Sons, New York 1972.

9. Gusdorf, *La Parole.*

10. Gusdorf, *La découverte de soi.*

11. Marc Orasion, *Death and Then What,* Paulist/Newman Press, Paramus, N. J. 1969.

12. Eliane Amado Lévy-Valensi, *La Communication,* P.U.F., Paris 1967.

Chapter 2

1. Jacques Sarano, 'Il ou Toi?', *Présences* No. 82, 1st Term 1973.

2. Arnold Stocker, *Le Traitement moral des nerveux,* Beauchesne, Paris 1948.

3. René Allendy, *L'enfance méconnue,* Editions Mont-Blanc, Geneva 1946.

4. Carl R. Rogers, *On Becoming a Person*, Houghton Mifflin, Boston 1961.

5. William Brunat, *Autour de l'enfant malade*, Paul Derain, Lyon 1945.

6. Buber, op. cit.

7. Henriette Lefebvre, *Un 'Sauveur', le docteur Vittoz*.

8. Henri Fesquet, *La foi toute nue*, Grasset, Paris 1972.

Chapter 3

1. Sigmund Freud, *The Psychopathology of Everyday Life*, New American Library, New York 1952.

2. Paul Ricoeur, *Freud and Philosophy: An Essay on Interpretation*, Yale University Press, New Haven 1970.

3. Louis Kling, 'Das Kollektive Unbewusste im Leben von Sigmund Freud', *Grenzgebiete der Wissenschaft*, Kral, Abensberg April–June 1971.

4. Jacques Dor, 'Discussion d'une conférence de Marcel Arnaud: Le concept psycho-somatique, ses incidences en chirurgie', *Marseille chirurgical*, Marseilles, November–December 1955.

5. Joseph Gander, 'Die Entwicklung der Medizin von Virchow zu Tournier', *Civitas* No. 9.

6. Jacques Monod, *Chance and Necessity*, Knopf, New York 1971.

7. Charles Baudouin, *De l'instinct à l'esprit*, Delachaux & Niestlé, Neuchâtel 1970.

8. William James, *Varieties of Religious Experience*, Modern Library, New York.

9. Alexis Carrel, *Reflections on Life*, Hamish Hamilton 1952.

10. Viktor Frankl, *La psychothérapie et son image de l'homme*, Resma, Paris 1970.

11. Louis Pouyanne, 'Le médecin et la vie chrétienne', *Les Deux Cités* No. 4, Editions Réforme, Paris.

12. Maurice Zundel, 'L'homme existe-t-il?', *Conférences du Cénacle Libanais* No. 2, Beirut 1966.

13. Buber, op. cit.

14. Bertrand de Jouvenel, *Arcadie*, Harper & Row, New York 1973.

15. Denis V. Martin, *Faith and Spiritual Healing*, Epworth Press.

16. Frankl, op. cit.

17. Buber, op. cit.

18. René A. Spitz, *The First Year of Life*, International Univ. Press 1965.

Chapter 4

1. Jean Sarkissoff, 'L'utilisation en psychothérapie de la voix maternelle foetale selon Tomatis', *Médecine et Hygiène* No. 1082, Geneva, 12 December 1973.

2. Lorenz, op. cit.

3. Spitz, op. cit.

4. O. Rank, *The Trauma of Birth*, Harcourt Brace & World, NY 1929.

5. Susumu Akahoshi, *Incurability and 'Basic Mistrust'*, Lecture delivered at the 1973 Conference on the Medicine of the Person, at Bossey. See also 'Agape and Eros', *Paul Tournier's Medicine of the Whole Person*, Word Books, Waco, Texas 1973.

6. E. Erikson, *Childhood and Society*, Norton, NY 1963.

7. H. Segal, *Introduction to the Work of Melanie Klein*, Basic Books, New York 1964.

8. F. Leboyer, *La naissance sans violence*, Le Seuil, Paris 1974.

9. Spitz, op. cit.

10. M. L. Levine & A. Bell, 'The Treatment of Colic in Infancy by the Use of the Pacifier', *Journal de Pédiatrie*, No. 37, 1960.

11. Spitz, op. cit.

12. Sarkissoff, op. cit.

13. Michael Balint, *The Doctor, his Patient, and the Illness*, 2nd edn revised and enlarged, Pitman Medical 1968.

14. Segal, op. cit.

15. Jan van der Hoeven, 'Medicine of the Whole Person and the Child', *Paul Tournier's Medicine of the Whole Person*, Word Books, Waco, Texas 1973.

16. Jean Sarkissoff, *Psychanalyse et Spiritualité*, Editions 'Etre Libre', Brussels.

17. Paul Plattner, 'The Person of the Doctor in the Medicine of the Whole Person', *Paul Tournier's Medicine of the Whole Person*, Word Books, Waco, Texas 1973.

18. Arthur Jores, 'The Diagonal Relationship Between the Doctor and the Patient in a Medicine of the Whole Person', *Paul Tournier's Medicine of the Whole Person*, Word Books, Waco, Texas 1973.